WHEELCHAIR CHAMPIONS

A History of Wheelchair Sports

by HARRIET MAY SAVITZ

AN AUTHORS GUILD BACKINPRINT.COM EDITION

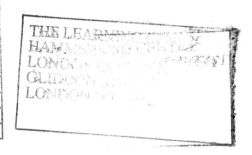
WHEELCHAIR CHAMPIONS
A History of Wheelchair Sports

AN AUTHORS GUILD BACKINPRINT.COM EDITION
Published by iUniverse, Inc.

For information address:
iUniverse, Inc.
2021 Pine Lake Road, Suite 100
Lincoln, NE 68512
www.iuniverse.com

Originally published by John Day

All photographs in this book are by Jim McGowan, with
the exception of those on page 20 and on page 26, bottom.
The photograph on page 26 is by Dreher Richards, and is used
through the courtesy of H. Charles Ryder.

SUMMARY: Delineates the development of sports for the
physically handicapped using wheelchairs and includes
the personal experiences of many paraplegics and quadriplegics.

ISBN-13: 978-0-595-38522-5
ISBN-10: 0-595-38522-2

Printed in the United States of America

WHEELCHAIR CHAMPIONS

INTRODUCTION

Whenever it is spring, I think of the Wheelchair Games and those who competed in them. For years I traveled with many of the teams, writing in books what I experienced in wheelchair sports. Wherever we visited, in whatever motel or hotel, or restaurant, we had to deal with steps, narrow doorways and uncomfortable expressions of other people. Wherever we traveled, we reminded others that accessibility and attitudes were the problems, not the disabled.

Wheelchair sports brought the disabled out into the community in masses. In the years since the publication of this first history of the athletes and trainers, the coaches and therapists, of all the pioneers in this disabled movement, there has been a steady development of sports involving the disabled and an expansion of the competitions. Throughout these past years, I have received numerous requests for this book by trainers, therapists, teachers, librarians, and the disabled themselves. I feel now as I felt then when I wrote the book, that each generation should know the struggles and accomplishments of the pioneers who determined that the disabled could establish themselves as self-fulfilled active citizens.

Nothing has been changed in the text. Jim McGowan, the photographer for the first printing, himself a quadriplegic-amputee, offered the original cover for the book. Wheelchair Champions is a history of the courageous and determined disabled and able-bodied who dared to believe that those in wheelchairs could be competitive in sports as well as in all areas of life.

Harriet May Savitz—2006

Please note the references to organizations and suggested reading material in the back of this book are outdated. Now new sources can be found in the wonderful world of the Internet.

ACKNOWLEDGMENTS

I would like to thank H. Charles Ryder for never saying no to my constant requests for information. Through the frustrating moments when facts were hiding like children playing games, he was always there to guide me. Because of his encouragement and unending support, I was able to compose this book.

My gratitude goes to Cliff Crase, who cooperated by digging into the generous files of *Sports 'n Spokes* for addresses and facts, using the resources of his fine magazine to aid my pursuit.

My constant appreciation goes to the librarians at the William Jeanes Memorial Library. If the information I needed was not within their reach, they quickly found it elsewhere.

The author holds great affection for Edward B. Davenport and L. Leah Rutter, both of whom shared their knowledge and gave constant support through the hours of research that gradually multiplied into years.

And then, of course, there is Jim McGowan, who wheeled over miles of rough turf to get pictures of the athletes, and with his fine sensitive eye picked up scenes that escaped the written word. His belief that this book deserved to be written, and his gentle but constant reminder that it must be, inspired me to continue.

The most rewarding part of writing WHEELCHAIR CHAMPIONS was the love I felt while all those athletes and coaches around the country worked together, searching in their attics and basements for records long stored away, to make this book possible.

To Eph—
and the exciting mountains still to climb.

To My Dad—
and the joy he gets in climbing them.

CONTENTS

The greatest thrill I have had in wheelchair sports is to stand on the first-place pedestal at the Paralympics and hear "The Star-Spangled Banner" being played and see the American flag being raised because I have performed well for my country. This has happened to me in London, Rome, and Tokyo, and the goose pimples and tears rolling down my cheeks are always there, no matter how often I win.

No athlete can gain any more satisfaction than to know that he has won for his country.

—Saul Welger, 1976
original member of Pan Am
Wheelchair Basketball Team

THE NINETEEN FORTIES

Who is the wheelchair sports athlete? He is the swimmer streaking across the pool. He is the archer tugging at the bow. He is the track and field competitor tossing javelins, hurling the discus, challenging the past records of wheelchair racers. He is the basketball player "putting one in," the weight lifter struggling to make a new record. The wheelchair athlete is one of the thousands of competitors who join wheelchair sports competitions around the country.

Wheelchair sports began toward the end of World War II. Many soldiers returned home from that war paralyzed from the waist down; they were called paraplegics. Others came home without legs; they were called amputees. Still others came home without the use of either arms or legs; they were known as quadriplegics.

Basketball, the first organized wheelchair competition sport. Scene at left is from a 1976 game between the Bordentown (New Jersey) Elks and the Philadelphia Easter Seal Paranauts.

Before World War II, there had been alive virtually no significant population of the disabled. Paraplegics who had spinal-cord injuries rarely survived. In World War I, three-quarters of the eighteen hundred casualties with spinal-cord injuries died on the battlefields or in the hospitals of France. Ninety percent of the remainder died within a year after their return to the United States. All the rest died within eighteen months, from kidney failure.

But World War II brought with it modern technology and miracle drugs. Because of the new wonder-drug penicillin, some twenty-five hundred spinal-cord injured veterans survived to return to their homes. In the years that followed, the numbers would grow to well over twenty thousand who had survived spinal-cord injuries.

In the mid nineteen forties the outside world—the world outside the Veterans Administration Hospital—was beginning to stir to the needs of the physically disabled. So many boys had returned home in wheelchairs, with some form of physical disability—too many to ignore.

Special wheelchairs were soon to be built and designed. The first wheelchairs had been wooden and noncollapsible. Those who used them couldn't have them transported—folded up to put into a car. Traveling, going anywhere, was impossible. Without the ability to travel and move about, the disabled were not part of society.

Then two innovative men, one in a wooden wheelchair, became friends, and out of that friendship came the fold-up wheelchair. Harry C. Jennings, Sr., was an engineer; Herbert A. Everest was the man in the wooden wheelchair. Herbert Everest also was an engineer, but he had become paralyzed when he suffered a broken back during a cave-in. At that time the doctors felt he would live for no more than two years. Contrary to medical predictions, he surprised the profession by surviving for many years.

Harry Jennings wanted to do something for his paralyzed friend. He wanted Herbert Everest to be able to get around, to travel, to have mobility. So he designed the lightweight, collapsible, metal wheelchair, which could easily be folded up and put in the back of a car. Harry Jennings' wheelchair would bring the greatest change in attitude to the disabled population. Now they would be able to travel to their jobs, to go about, to be again part of an outside world they had once enjoyed. Wheelchair sports would become possible because of this flexible wheelchair. Harry C. Jennings and Herbert Everest joined forces to form a company that was to become one of the largest designers and producers of wheelchairs in this country.

There was still much to be done. Automobiles with hand controls were just coming into production and use, but not fast enough for the desperate disabled veterans who were not sure just how long they had to live. Two stories persist depicting the frustration of those confined to hospitals. In one case, a paraplegic, anxious to drive but with no hand controls available, persuaded another paraplegic to accompany him. One drove while the other sat on the floor and worked the foot pedals with his hands at the driver's command.

In the second incident, a quadriplegic, impatient to drive his new car but again without the necessary hand controls, enlisted the aid of a blind patient. The blind patient drove while the "quad" (quadriplegic) sat alongside and gave instructions as to when to go, stop, and turn.

These were the moments of insanity, when disabled veterans, unsure of their future, feeling that death was only a moment away, plunged head-first into living. But even just living, just getting by, held obstacles for the disabled veteran: architectural barriers, limited medical care, the handicap of ignorance—and everywhere were narrow doorways and steps, steps, steps.

The more doctors at veterans' hospitals saw the disabled filling the hospitals, the more they knew something must be done to help the confused young men—some of them still boys—pick up their lives again.

At first the veterans were kept busy at the VA (Veterans Administration) hospitals with therapy—with newly fitted braces, with getting to know their new means of transportation, the wheelchair.

Still, the disabled ex-GI's kept asking questions. What did people in wheelchairs do for recreation? How did they participate in sports? Those who had become disabled through falls, through accidents, through disease, shook their heads and could only answer, "We don't know."

That's the way it was as World War II drew to a close. It was a world where wheelchairs had their limits and where those in wheelchairs had their limits, too. It was a world in which the federal government was just beginning to realize the inadequacy of its programs for the physically disabled.

One day, while wheeling around the gym in a veterans' hospital, a young GI picked up a basketball, which happened to be lying around, and began to dribble, then wheel his chair, then dribble again. Then he shot the ball toward the basket.

It missed. When he lifted both hands to shoot the ball, the young veteran started to fall forward, his body tilting, spilling out of the chair from lack of balance.

It seemed impossible to shoot from a wheelchair. The young veteran tried again. The basketball hit near the net. Again he tipped out. His balance was gone. So was his power. But his aim—his hand-eye coordination—was as good as ever!

Again he tried a shot, and this time he concentrated on balance, on staying in the chair. Time after time, he kept the ball shooting toward the net, to the side of it, under it, then, unbelievably, into the net. Excitement began to stir inside him.

Gradually he found a few other veterans who were interested in playing basketball. They began to dribble, to shoot, to wheel a little faster, to play around at racing each other across the court, maneuvering around each other's wheelchairs.

There weren't enough veterans at the hospital for two teams, so some AB's (able-bodied veterans) got into wheelchairs. The disabled players found they were beating the AB's, because they were used to their wheelchair, because they had acquired speed in wheeling, and sometimes just because they were tougher. In order to survive, they had to be.

While World War II veterans were pioneering wheelchair basketball, another type of pioneering was going on in the United States. Major Howard A. Rusk was working with sick and injured patients in the hospital at Jefferson Barracks, Missouri. Major Rusk organized a convalescent rehabilitation program for soldier patients who were recovering from their wounds. In a short time, all army, air force, and navy hospitals had adopted similar programs.

As greater thought was given to the needs of the disabled veteran after his return to his home and family, groups of military officers were sent to the Institute for the Crippled and Disabled in New York City for training programs in rehabilitation.

The United States had awakened suddenly to the fact that it must restore its disabled veterans—all disabled veterans—to far better living conditions. They had to be taught to be independent again, to drive automobiles, to get used to their artificial limbs, or braces, to learn to eat with hooks that served as hands, to get jobs, and to believe in themselves again.

The disabled veterans, paralyzed and amputees, were waking up, too. They were experimenting in gyms throughout the United States, feeling their way in their wheelchairs, getting the touch of the basketball, learning to judge the distance, a new distance from the chair to the net. They were learning, too, how to control their balance while shooting.

Gyms in veterans' hospitals grew active with wheels spinning across courts, balls thumping against tough young chests, chairs zigzagging across the slick floors.

Gradually, audiences began to gather to sit on the sidelines, watching, applauding, cheering their teams on. Rehabilitation workers, families of the competitors, doctors, nurses, and the curious soon filled the stands.

The teams expanded as new faces joined the practice sessions. Players disabled by polio, paraplegics who weren't veterans, began filling in on the teams and then joining as regulars.

It became easier to get two teams together, then four, and still the wheelchair basketball games improved, and audiences grew. The day came when large numbers of veterans were ready to leave the hospital. Hundreds went immediately to rehabilitation centers where many took courses preparing them for a trade; others returned to school.

Wheelchair basketball continued. It had spread to rehabilitation centers where disabled veterans were taking courses.

Several wheelchair basketball teams had already begun to tour the country, spreading interest in their sport. For the first time, wheelchair basketball took on a truly competitive aspect at the Birmingham Veterans Hospital in Van Nuys, California, when a set of official wheelchair basketball rules was written by Mr. Rynearson, the assistant athletic director at Birmingham, who coached and originated the PVA (Paralyzed Veterans of America) Athletic Club, which later became the Flying Wheels.

At one time, the Flying Wheels of Van Nuys had as their coach Pop Brown, a World War I paraplegic. They would go on to establish a record in wheelchair basketball second to none. They became national champions seven times and won for five consecutive years from 1960 to 1964. In 1965 and 1966, the Flying Wheels finished in second place, thus setting another national record of having played in seven consecutive championships. The championship basketball team was holder of the longest winning

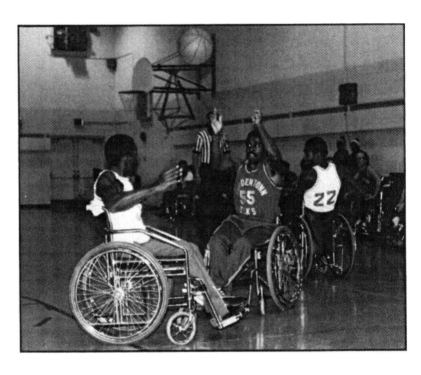

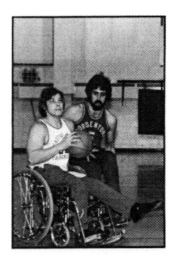

Photo sequence shows scenes from a 1976 game between the Bordentown (New Jersey) Elks and the Philadelphia Easter Seal Paranauts.

streak, forty-four games without defeat, and of still another record—winning eighteen straight games in national tournament play. In the exciting, experimental days of the forties, the Van Nuys team introduced the new sport to the paraplegic patients at the United States Naval Hospital in Corona, California. And about the same time that the Flying Wheels were paving their trail of glory, patients at Cushing General Hospital in Massachusetts began to explore the possibilities of wheelchair basketball.

From Kansas City, Missouri, came another team, the Pioneers. One of the first hometown nonveteran teams, these pioneers urged disabled citizens to participate and compete in wheelchair basketball. The Brooklyn Whirlaways, the Minneapolis Gophers of Minnesota, the Gizz Kids from Illinois, and the Bulova Watchmakers of Woodside, Long Island, New York, journeyed into the cities to find more players to bring out to the courts.

The wheelchair basketball sports world grew ever wider, reaching out to engage the interest of others who were newly disabled. The St. Louis Rams of Missouri and the Charioteers of Queens, New York, arrived on the scene as wheelchair exhibition teams increased. Something new had been born and was flourishing, something that had never before been seen in the world.

In 1948, there were eight wheelchair basketball teams in the United States. (In the next twenty-five years, this would grow to include seventeen conferences, more than one hundred teams, and more than fifteen hundred active participants.) Veterans were now leaving the rehabilitation centers, having completed their vocational and educational courses, ready now to contribute to society.

Thousands of disabled young men left the centers eager to find jobs. Most first tried to find a place to live. The disabled found this wasn't easy. There were always steps that prevented a wheelchair's access. Sometimes landlords looked at the wheelchair as if they were afraid of it. Many landlords made it clear that they doubted the disabled could pay the rent; after all, who would hire them? Others even worried about what their other tenants would say. And then there were those who just looked with eyes of pity. Always the wheelchair seemed to be on the other side of a closed door.

Job hunting was just as difficult. Employers seemed uneasy when interviewing the disabled veteran, vague when they turned him down. Too many businesses had steps without ramps. Employment agencies were not accessible. Steps and stairways kept the wheelchair out. The stares of the curious kept the disabled out, too.

At a VA hospital in a rehabilitation center, the veteran was one of many. In the city, job hunting, apartment hunting, facing the able-bodied and their fears, their ignorance, the disabled ex-GI began to feel he was different. It was only because he was made to feel different. Inside he was the same. Inside he had dreams and hopes. He wanted to tell everyone that, but no one seemed to want to listen. And even if someone did hear him—would the person understand? The returned disabled veteran was plagued by disappointment and depression.

But there was still wheelchair basketball, acting as a beacon for many through all the frustration. Somehow the days were bearable when the nights held their weekly practice sessions.

Wheelchair basketball, however, had its own set of obstacles. The teams found it difficult to get school gyms. School boards were cautious. Wheelchairs might mar the gym floor. It was even a task to reserve a recreation-center basketball court for this new type of sport. Few had heard of it before; even fewer cared. But the players practiced anyway, wherever and whenever they got a chance, because when playing basketball, each of them was part of a team again. To preserve this new form of competition, wheelchair basketball teams sometimes traveled five and six hours at a time, just to find another basketball team to play. Only the determination of the players kept the competitions alive.

About this time, the University of Illinois started experimenting with some new ideas about the physically disabled. Tim Nugent, director of student rehabilitation at the university, had begun a program called the Division of Rehabilitation Education Services. The goal of this service organization was to enable those qualified who were severely disabled or had a permanent physical disability to acquire a college education. For too many years, the disabled had been hustled off to institutions or kept in secluded private homes, seldom to have the chance to venture into the outside world again. Here was a new approach, and a man whose program encouraged the disabled not only to "join society again" but to go on to higher education, to achieve and excel.

The program, just beginning at the Galesburg Division of the University of Illinois, offered the physically disabled transportation to the university, medical care, physical therapy, functional training counseling, recreation and athletics, services for the blind and deaf, occupational therapy. Hundreds of disabled students would find their way to Tim Nugent's program and bring their hopes and dreams to his doorstep. Because of him, the University of Illinois would have more physically disabled graduates than any other college in the country.

The Division of Rehabilitation Education Services seemed to be only the beginning when it came to the needs of the disabled as far as Tim Nugent was concerned. Delta Sigma Omicron, a rehabilitation-service fraternity at the University of Illinois, was formed about this time. The fraternity consisted of students with physical disabilities. Delta Sigma Omicron sponsored Tim Nugent's first wheelchair basketball tournament, which was held in 1949. The team that represented the University of Illinois and would claim much fame in future years as superb athletes, was named the Gizz Kids. In years to come, the Gizz Kids would add baseball to their list of sports, and they and Delta Sigma Omicron would donate over $45,000 to various charities from the proceeds of their games.

But back in 1949, when Tim Nugent, the Gizz Kids, and Delta Sigma Omicron involved themselves in the first national wheelchair basketball tournament, wheelchair basketball and all wheelchair sports were in their infancy.

Things were happening quickly now. Tim Nugent and the Gizz Kids were organizing the National Wheelchair Basketball Association (NWBA). They developed a rule book that set up guidelines for the formation of local conferences with a minimum membership of three teams. Top teams in each conference qualified for regional tournaments, and winners of regional and / or sectional tournaments advanced to the national tournament.

Member teams of the NWBA would in future years contribute over one million dollars to the National Paraplegia Foundation, the National Polio Fund, United States Cerebral Palsy, and other such foundations.

Now there were five conferences: Midwest, Eastern, Pacific Coast, Southern, and Northwest. And the competition was fierce! No longer was it a question of a sport played by people thrown together during "fun time for the disabled." There were rules, regulations, qualifying games, and an order to the tournaments. The six teams that played in the original tournament were Chicago (Illinois) Cats, Evansville (Indiana) Rockets, Hannibal (Missouri) Rolling Rockets, Kansas City (Missouri) Rolling Pioneers, Minneapolis (Minnesota) Rolling Gophers, and the University of Illinois Gizz Kids.

Among the notable coaches of the Gizz Kids team would be Stan Labanowich, who later became commissioner of the National Wheelchair Basketball Association.

With a few exceptions, the NWBA rules are the same as those of the NCAA (National Collegiate Athletic Association), which able-bodied players follow. A player is restricted to two pushes on his wheelchair while holding the ball in his lap. After those two pushes on the hand rims of his wheelchair, he must dribble or bounce the ball at least once. If he doesn't do so, he will be called for a traveling violation. Another rule that has been changed from standard NCAA regulations is the amount of time the player is allowed in the "free-throw lane": three seconds for a running player, six seconds for a wheeling player. The wheelchair uses up that extra time in maneuvering around the other players.

A wheelchair basketball player must be careful not to raise himself off the seat of his chair. If, in the heat and speed of the game, he does this, it constitutes a physical advantage foul, which is treated as a technical foul, but with no free throw awarded. Three such violations and he's out of the game. This regulation can be responsible for many a good but hasty player retiring to the sidelines.

Much to the surprise of audiences attending wheelchair basketball games for the first time, the game is played on a regulation-size basketball court; the basket is the same height; the foul line, the same distance.

There has been, however, a classification, set up in a national meeting by a representative group of members from all the teams in the conferences, that prevents any team from being unfairly overloaded with highly muscle-powered wheelchair players. Because disabilities vary, because one member of a team might be paralyzed from the waist down, another from the chest, another an amputee with quick mobility and excellent muscle power and balance, players are separated into three classes: I, II, and III. A Class III player may be an amputee or someone polio-disabled who nevertheless has good muscle power. Perhaps the post-polio player may merely limp when he gets out of his wheelchair. Many people are stunned when they see some Class III players get out of their chairs and walk away. Some amputees will wear their artificial limb when playing; others will not. In order to play wheelchair basketball, a player must be ineligible to play NCAA basketball because of some form of disability. Cases of bone disease, bicycle injuries that damage hips, and mild polio all fit into the Class III category. A Class III player definitely has the advantage over those in the other classes of disabilities because he is the least disabled. He has a value of three points on the court.

A Class II player has the second-highest level of mobility and has a value of two points on the court.

Class I technically has the most limitation and the highest level of disability. Class I players are always fighting their loss of balance, and must constantly struggle to stay in the chair. Seat belts are not used in wheelchair basketball in the United States. Players are much safer tumbling out of their chairs and falling free of the chair; they seldom get hurt. If a player falls and he is in the center of the action (falling can happen in all three classes), the game will be stopped and the player helped back into his chair. But if a player falls from his chair when he is away from the play, he'll try to get back into the chair on his own. Usually, he can slide backward up into the chair. If he has difficulty, he'll have to wait until the game moves his way again or there is a time-out called. Class I has some powerful shooting players whose basketball scoring is constantly feared. A Class I player has a point value of one on the court.

In the mid seventies, a twelve-point system was developed to allow a more severely handicapped player more exposure and a chance to play on the first team. No team could have players with more than twelve points on the court at one time and no team could have more than three Class III players. These rules insure fair treatment for all types of disabilities and make certain that all the physically disabled have a chance to play. Coaches are careful of this, constantly checking the floor to make sure that their point totals are correct. If not, they will be called for a team foul and penalized.

Each player is required to have a strap at the back of his legs, secured from one foot pedal to the other. This is to prevent one or both of the legs from slipping off the foot pedal during the competition and causing injury to the player. It also prevents a player with muscle power in his legs from pushing—an unfair advantage.

Life began to broaden for all the physically disabled as a bigger picture came into view, the existence of wheelchair basketball competition and traveling with the teams to compete in tournaments around the country.

In 1948, Tim Nugent started wheelchair football in the Division of Rehabilitation Education Services at the University of Illinois. Two teams—the Blue Streaks and the White Flashes—competed against one another on Saturday mornings in the armory. In 1960, a third football team— the Golds—was formed. Chairs with heavy construction were especially built for wheelchair football, for this was a game of "smashing contact," speed, and agility. It required the toughest of wheelchairs and the toughest of men.

Wheelchair football is played according to NCAA rules, with a few important modifications:

1. Tackling consists of touching the ball carrier (not the wheelchair) above the knees with two hands simultaneously.

2. Blocking is permissible by ramming the wheel-

chair into the opponent's wheelchair from a front angle. Blocking into the large wheel constitutes "clipping."

3. All players on the team are eligible pass receivers.

4. A team must gain fifteen instead of ten yards for the first down.

5. On tries for extra points, two points are awarded for a successful run, and one for a successful pass. Tries are taken from the three-yard line.

6. A kick in wheelchair football is simulated by throwing a ball downfield. The kicking team must declare its intention to kick to the defensive team through the referee before breaking the huddle.

Some great football stars have left legendary records: George Veenstra, Golds, record 2,857 total yards passing, 1964-70; Paul Jarboe, Whites, record 830 total yards passing, 1968-74; Tom Brown, Blues, total yards rushing 928 (6.1 yards per rush) 1966-71; Tom Brown, Blues, 267 total points scored, 1966-71; George Veenstra, Golds, 4,351 total yards, 1964-70.

Wheelchair football would grow more slowly than other wheelchair sports because it needed a large indoor area with a hard surface. It could not be played on grass.

In the late nineteen-forties, thoughts of other ways of competing were beginning to stir among physically disabled athletes. It seemed only natural for them to begin to ask each other, "What else is there to do in sports for the physically disabled athlete besides play basketball or football?"

News came to this country of a neurosurgeon named Ludwig Guttman, founder of the Stoke-Mandeville Spinal Cord Injury Center in England. He had started experimenting with a group of twenty-six physically disabled archery players, and then had tried lawn bowling, table tennis, shot put, javelin, club throwing, with snooker, swimming, and fencing to follow in the future.

Was it possible to do all these things while confined to a wheelchair? To throw a javelin? To swim? These haunting questions stirred the disabled. Many of them had earlier been good swimmers. They began to wonder, Why not now?

In time Dr. Guttman's competitions would come to be known as the Stoke-Mandeville Games; they would be held annually. The Dutch would start contesting with the British in these new forms of wheelchair competition; the Stoke-Mandeville Games would become international.

The forties closed with a new awareness in the American population. Through increasing wheelchair competition, Americans awoke to the fact that they had been neglecting an important part of their society, and that they were totally ignorant of the needs of the physically disabled.

THE NINETEEN FIFTIES

The fifties exploded with new breakthroughs that affected the lives of the disabled. The Korean War compounded the number of disabled veterans. A second generation of antibiotics was discovered, and more lives were saved. Dr. Howard Rusk took his wartime experience and his plans to New York City, to build the famous Rusk Institute for Rehabilitation Medicine at New York University Medical Center.

Hearings on rehabilitation began in the House of Representatives in 1953. Rehabilitation centers—such as the Craig Center of Denver, Colorado; the Kessler Institute in West Orange, New Jersey; the Sister Kenny Institute in Minneapolis, Minnesota; the Rancho Los Amigos in Los Angeles, California; the Rehabilitation Institute of Chicago, Illinois; and the Magee Memorial Rehabilitation Center in Philadelphia, Pennsylvania—began to spring up around the country. The Social Security Act was amended to protect the insurance benefits of workers who became disabled. The nineteen fifties became a developmental stage in the history of the disabled. Rehabilitation facilities were

Archery competitors (Montreal team) at the First National Wheelchair Athletic Games at Adelphi University, 1957.

improved and expanded by using basic grant funds.

The fifties brought change in wheelchair sports, also. There was talk of a national wheelchair sports competition. Benjamin H. Lipton of the Joseph Bulova School of Watchmaking had been inquiring about wheelchair competitions in this country. He had been a veterans' counselor at a VA hospital, where he first saw wheelchair basketball. He had served in the hospital's administration during World War II, as well as in the reserves. He had a master's degree in counseling and had retired from the military service with the rank of major.

In the early fifties, Ben Lipton came to the Joseph Bulova School of Watchmaking as director. This school had once had as its slogan, "To serve those who served us." Its great benefits were intended for those veterans who had returned disabled from World War II. However, as the years passed, the slogan was changed to, "To serve those who need a chance." Thus disabled civilians also benefited from the tuition-free school.

Ben Lipton, after thorough searching, had found that aside from wheelchair basketball and football, there was no other type of wheelchair athletics in this country. It was about this time that Dr. Ludwig Guttman, the pioneer in wheelchair sports in England, came to the United States. During his stay in this country, he visited Ben Lipton at the Bulova School. They discussed the possibility of enlisting the cooperation of the United States in entering wheelchair international competition.

Ben Lipton came away from that meeting with much to think about and much to decide. His involvement in the Bulova School of Watchmaking was total. Besides being director, he was coach of the Bulova Watchmakers Basketball Team, and administrator of the Arde Bulova Memorial Scholarship Program, a program that has trained more than a thousand handicapped men from the United States and other countries as watchmakers, repairers, and precision-instrument technicians.

Ben Lipton's life was busy. It would become even busier, sometimes hectic, and incredibly exciting after he reached his final decision.

It was about this time that Pan American World Airways took a big step into the circle of wheelchair sports. In the early fifties, tragedy had struck the family of James McGuire, then head of the accounting department of Pan Am. His daughter Patsy was stricken with polio. Patsy at first used a wheelchair to get around, then braces, then a cane. James McGuire's boss, John S. Woodbridge, then Pan Am's comptroller, happened to attend the semifinals match in Brooklyn of the national wheelchair basketball tournament. The Brooklyn Whirlaways and Queens Charioteers were competing. As they displayed their skill, the growing new world of wheelchair basketball opened to John Woodbridge. He became curious, interested. He asked questions of the team members. In the back of his mind was always Patsy McGuire.

John Woodbridge found that some of the members of the Charioteers and Whirlaways were actually employed by his company. He went to work immediately, recruiting men from both teams. He trained them in accounting, and put them in James McGuire's department.

The men formed the first basketball team composed only of employees of a single sponsoring company, the Pan Am

Jets. A large company was actively involving itself in the potential of wheelchair sports, and was discovering thrilling yet unexplored possibilities.

The Pan Am Jets trained hard, three nights a week and on Saturday and Sunday mornings. Pan Am paid the fee for the use of the Forest Hills High School in Queens, New York, which had an excellent gym for basketball and a big field for track and field sports.

The company also hired a special track and field coach to teach the Jets how to throw the javelin and shot put. The Jets worked hard and vowed that they would extend themselves to the fullest limits of their abilities. The Pan Am Jets did not forget Patsy McGuire. She became their team mascot. At that time, Patsy was undergoing a series of operations, and the Jets visited her in the hospital, bringing her miniature trophies and jackets which they had made up especially for her. James McGuire continued to help out with the team on their trips to competitions, traveling with them whenever possible. Patsy remembers that her father always said that the disabled were the best of his employees, the most eager to get the job done.

The coach of the Pan Am Jets was Bill Condon, a junior accountant for Pan Am. The manager of the team was Tom Ford. When Bill Condon left Pan Am in 1958, Junius Kellogg, an ex-Harlem Globetrotter, became coach. Junius, a former Manhattan College basketball star, became a paraplegic due to an automobile accident. He and Ford stayed with the team until it was disbanded in 1964.

The hard work of the Pan Am Jets paid off. The ten original Jets achieved a remarkable record of victories. They defeated the twenty-four other United States wheelchair basketball teams in their first year of play. In 1955, the Jets went to London to participate in the International Paralympics (so named because all the participants were paraplegics). In London, they defeated entries from fifteen other countries to become the world-champion wheelchair basketball team. The Jets would hold that title for five successive years.

The Pan Am Jets and their success sparked a flurry of new teams. The Jets were in demand all over the world, playing demonstration games and competing. They brought with them a new image for the disabled—the image of a winner.

Now many veterans and nonveteran athletes in the United States began to get ready for large-scale wheelchair sports. They conditioned their bodies. They trained for speed, racing down front sidewalks and driveways. They went to local high schools and found swimming instructors who were willing to help them exercise and practice. They found empty parking lots and coached themselves, and strengthened arms that already boasted muscles. They bought javelins and field equipment; they outfitted their wheelchairs for racing, and they waited to hear news of what this country would decide to do.

When the United States was ready, there were hundreds of disabled athletes ready, too. In 1957, the United States, under the guidance of Ben Lipton, with the sponsorship of the Joseph Bulova School of Watchmaking, the Paralyzed Veterans of America, and Long Island's Adelphi University, held the first National Wheelchair Games in this country.

The Paralyzed Veterans of America (a nonprofit, non-

Right: *Ben Lipton, Chairman of the National Wheelchair Athletic Association since 1958, elected to the NWAA Hall of Fame, 1974.*

Bottom: *Paraplegic Alonzo Wilkins,* left, *first superstar of U.S. wheelchair sports, with Charles Ryder, who wrote the first set of rules for wheelchair games. (Photo from the Third Pennsylvania Wheelchair Games, 1970)*

Opposite: *Double amputee Russell Stone, tossing shot. (Photo 1976)*

Dreher Richards

sectarian, interracial organization) had formed in 1947 a national organization, with a publication called the *Paraplegia News*.

When, in 1957, the "Nationals" opened in this country, they were initiated, designed, and organized by three men—Ben Lipton, Charlie Ryder, and Joe Crafa. Charlie Ryder and Joe Crafa were both from Adelphi University.

Charlie Ryder had been with Bulova on a part-time basis since 1955, when Bulova offered a fellowship program to Adelphi University. The fellowship was to be given to a physical-education student to help develop a broader recreation program for the handicapped at the Bulova School. Charlie was selected and began working during the following years to build better recreation programs for the students at Bulova. Because of his involvement, Bulova began experimenting with badminton, volley ball, table tennis, archery, and with tournament play.

In order to prepare for the various competitions at the National Wheelchair Games, tests had been given in advance to students at the Bulova School. It was important to determine how each event would be performed. The circumstances of these games were unique. There was no precedent to follow in this country, because nothing like this had ever been attempted before. New rules and events, to be altered and improved in the future, were devised for safety and fairness.

Adelphi University readied its grounds for the oncoming competitions—in darts, archery, table tennis, javelin, basketball, free throw, the 60-yard dash on a macadam racetrack, and the 240-yard shuttle relay.

Sixty-three competitors showed up to attend the first National Wheelchair Games. Though the disabled were enthusiastic and anxious to join the competitions, few had actually traveled before. The reality of getting to the Nationals by car, bus, train, or plane discouraged many from participating. Only a few states were represented, but it didn't matter to those who attended. It was a beginning. The events took on a surprisingly international flavor with the appearance of a four-man team, the Wheelchair Wonders, from Montreal, Canada.

Competitors included vocational and university students, gainfully employed adults, teen-agers, patients in VA hospitals and in other hospitals and rehabilitation centers. The sports participants were physically disabled by paraplegia, polio, illness, wartime wounds, accidents, birth defects, and amputations.

Men and women did not compete against one another in these Nationals. All the contestants participated either as members of teams or as individuals who were graduates of a rehabilitation center or from an institution. Often a big van or bus would pull up bearing an institution's name. Many times it was the competitor's first experience traveling, sometimes even his first trip outside the institution.

Teams came representing vocational schools, rehabilitation centers, universities, and wheelchair sports clubs. All competitors were divided up into classes according to each athlete's disability. The teams often gave assistance to those who showed up individually for competition. It was not unusual to hear instructions shouted across the field: "Hey, follow up with that shot-put throw!" "You're not throwing that javelin right!" and "Go with the wind!" Physical therapists, under medical supervision, gave the athletes tests to determine how much muscle power they had in different parts of their bodies, classifying them accordingly.

There were coaches and assistants at the Nationals. That first time at Adelphi and for many years to come, the coaches and assistants were in charge of carrying field equipment, a box of tools to keep the wheelchairs together, and many times they were depended upon to return to their chairs competitors who had toppled out during hectic competition. The coaches also had to know how to keep a sharp eye on the stopwatch.

As wheelchair sports became more intense, so did the competitors. Rules were challenged; decisions on records were questioned; athletes showed up with cushions too high and chairs too low. But wheelchair sports adapted to the changes. The qualifications of the coaches grew tighter.

As the years went on, all officials were required to be members of the National Wheelchair Officials Association, to have had professional experience, and to take a written test in every event in which they officiated. Later, the National Wheelchair Officials Association (NWOA) would develop and implement standardized methods of training, certification, and rating of officials for local, regional, and national wheelchair sports competition.

But in 1957 at Adelphi, everything was in its infancy, its simplest form. It was a tough weekend for the new athlete. It seemed to be all things at once, meeting new friends, measuring skills against the skills of those he competed against, and adapting to strange surroundings.

The Adelphi weekend brought with it many unexpected

moments and produced its first national wheelchair-sports athletic star: Alonzo Wilkins.

A Korean War veteran, Alonzo had been injured in a freak accident during a rough storm at sea upon his return home from combat in Korea. The tossing waters and storm-wracked boat flung Alonzo against the railing of the boat, causing his injury. He became a paraplegic, unable to move from his waist down.

Upon graduating from the Bulova School of Watchmaking, Alonzo had stayed on at the school to work. He quickly became manager of the school's Bulova Watchmakers team and Mr. Lipton's right-hand man.

One of the fiercest and most outstanding paraplegic competitors wheelchair sports has known, Alonzo provided a challenge to all new competitors that first weekend and for many years to come. During his athletic career, Alonzo won gold medals in discus, javelin, slalom, singles and doubles table tennis. He became president of the Eastern Wheelchair Basketball Conference and represented the United States in its first competition in the Paralympics, held in Rome, Italy, in 1970.

In 1958, the year after the first Nationals, the National Wheelchair Athletic Association was organized. It governed all activities in wheelchair sports except wheelchair basketball, which had its own association. Membership in the association was open to all men and women wheelchair athletes and to officials and coaches, either involved or interested in wheelchair sports; there are also affiliate members. Members could range from thirteen to sixty-five years in age.

The National Wheelchair Athletic Committee was

formed soon afterward to direct the activities of the National Wheelchair Athletic Association (NWAA). The NWAC consisted of a chairman, twelve members, a medical advisory board, and later, in the seventies, sanctioned regional representatives. Each member was elected to a one-year term. The NWAC attended to record and rule changes, publishing and recording them. They maintained wheelchair athletic records and rules on claims to new records; they were responsible for the selection of sites for national meets, and they sanctioned official regional meets.

The committee was responsible for the selection of athletes who would represent the United States in international competition, including basketball. It was the selection of this great Paralympic team, which would travel to many European countries, that proved to be the highlight of many Nationals' awards banquets: the hushed silence at the banquet just before the United States team members were announced—and then with each name the thunderous applause, the tears, the embracing as another international athletic star was born.

Disabled competitors now traveled regularly to the annual Nationals, perfecting their skills, bringing back medals, earning acclaim from enlightened citizens in their hometowns.

The meets were developing as wheelchair sports grew. Track events now included 40-, 60-, and 100-yard dashes; 220- and 440-yard dashes; 880-yard and mile runs as distance races; 240- and 400-yard shuttle relays; and 880-yard and mile relays. Racing records were broken and new ones established as wheels spun and muscular arms pushed and strained.

The audience rose to a chorus of excitement as the gun sounded to start the athletes off. The crowds—the rooters, the friends, the loved ones—ignited with whistles, calls of encouragement: "Faster, faster!" "Come on, you can finish!" And then moments later, the exhausted silence at the end, while the audience and athletes joined in waiting for the winners to be announced.

In the field, the crowds marveled at the sweep of the discus across the field, and at the throw of the javelin. The power of the athletes who had spent many hours pushing their wheelchairs was obvious.

Archery, the silent sport, as champion archer Jack Whitman often referred to it, had its long moments of solid concentration. Hours seemingly would go by with the only sound the rustling of nearby trees. Arrows sought out the gold, the bull's-eye, as wheelchair archers like graceful warriors endured the heat of the summer sun in order to place, to win, to set a new record.

The International Ladies Shot Put . . . how easily some seemed to lift it, to toss it into the field! Only the flexed muscles, the perspiration dotting the forehead, the sound of the painful grunt as the thrust, the blending of energy and skill, gave evidence that this small ball of steel could drain the body of its energy. Often those watching could feel the tightness in their own bellies at that moment of trial when the shot put smacked into the ground.

The slalom was a race against time. It took the competitors through obstacles that brought thrills to the crowd. The courses, defined by flags, covered a minimum of 60 and a maximum of 80 yards and included at least each of the following: a jump onto a platform, a jump off a platform, a ramp on a platform, a ramp off a platform. The jump on and off the platform was done without a ramp. The wheelchair popped up and down in a position similar to the wheelie maneuver, balancing on the rear wheels, used by the disabled in jumping curbs. The slalom held a minimum of eight gates of flags, each 4 feet wide, not permanently fixed to the surface and set so that a test of agility was required. Slalom platforms were 6 inches high, 40 inches wide, and 40 inches long.

Athletes would tell later of the slalom's effects, of how their hearts beat faster at the anticipation, just as they would have at the top of a long ski slope. Those who attempted the slalom knew of its dangers.

Risks were not new to the disabled. Many enjoyed shocking the able-bodied by performing in their wheelchairs, taking unbelievable chances while doing so. Outside the competitions, the athletes could be seen going down steps in their wheelchairs (not recommended for anyone who is not an expert).

At one national event, a wheelchair athlete startled an entire town by accompanying an automobile through the main street during rush-hour traffic. The wheelchair rider, on the automobile driver's side, held on to the car door through its open window. There he was, riding along the street in his wheelchair, hanging on to the side door of the car which was being driven at a fairly high speed. It was dangerous and perhaps foolhardy, but it was another way that the disabled could say, "I'm not afraid."

If there were no rules concerning wheelchairs when it came to driving in city streets, there were rules during the competitions. Wheelchair sports were gaining sophistication. Regulations were changed and adopted to bring better accuracy and fairness to the sport. The list of competitors grew, and so did the list of competitions. Archery, dartchery (a combination of dart and target archery), basketball, fencing, field events (discus, javelin, club throw, shot put, lawn bowling, pentathlon, 60-yard dash), swimming (front freestyle, back freestyle, breaststroke), table tennis (singles and doubles), track events (40-yard dash—60-yard, 100-yard, 220-yard, 440-yard, 880-yard, and mile slalom), weight lifting.

The competitors in wheelchair sports learned more than how to compete. They had to acclimate themselves to constant change. They stayed at different hotels—some with ramps, some without; some with accessible bathrooms, some with none. They became accustomed to coping with unpredictable situations: swimming in a pool with a group of AB's (able-bodied) who would leave as soon as an amputee dipped into the water, or facing the stares in a restaurant as forty wheelchairs converged on the scene. The athletes—many of them pampered by overprotective parents, many just newly out of institutions or rehabilitation centers—were sometimes shocked, sometimes angry, often frustrated, but always they were being drawn into living.

In the fifties, fame began to court the wheelchair athletes in their hometowns. They were talked of on the radio, sometimes even seen on national TV; they were written about in the press. Frequently they were asked to make speeches and to give exhibitions of wheelchair sports. People would recognize them, stop them on the street, shake their hands, applaud their victories.

It was an exciting era for wheelchair sports. It was one of exploration and acclaim. One new team after another was developed, with coaches, helpers, and officials participating. It was the era of laughter, of fun, of trying, failing, and trying again.

Individuals Begin to Care

Henry Viscardi, Jr., borrowed eight thousand dollars in 1952, gave up a good job as personnel director, and in a vacant garage, started Abilities, Inc.

Viscardi, who had stumps for legs, believed that the physically disabled could work efficiently in industry. He was forty when he launched Abilities, Inc., with five disabled employees and an idea of manufacturing "anything." Today the organization has grown to occupy twenty landscaped acres at the Human Resources Center on Long Island, which is often referred to as "the campus."

Abilities, Inc., offers employment to those who might ordinarily be on welfare. A demonstration industrial and clerical work center, it provides work for over 175 disabled and retarded adults. Those employed put in a full eight hours a day and are responsible for providing their own transportation to and from the job.

Jobs vary from telephone communications, electronic and mechanical assembly work, to data processing, glass carving, and packaging. Over $4-million worth of business is produced at Abilities, Inc., each year.

The Human Resources School at the Long Island center offers a tuition-free education to those children who are severely disabled. Over two hundred such children attend the school, which provides a full academic curriculum to students who previously were thought to be homebound.

Founded in 1962, the school began with twenty-one children in one room at the Human Resources Center. In September 1965, a new building was opened; students on crutches, in wheelchairs, on litters, with braces and without legs, but with every kind of hope, came to take advantage of the fine academic curriculum and the facilities designed for those in wheelchairs.

There are nineteen classrooms in the school with special rooms for art, science, and homemaking. The high school juniors and seniors occupy the wings. The center has wider-than-usual aisles, piped-in music, excellent lighting, and customized workbenches. Sixty-seven percent of those graduating go on to college each year. Those who do not will have the training to enter the world of business and industry.

The Research and Program Development Institute, established in 1957, conducts research and sponsors projects in psychology, special education, and vocational rehabilitation. In an attempt to foster his belief that all men and women can achieve a measure of independence, Henry Viscardi has seen to it that the institute evaluates and trains 250 persons each year. The training center's program reaches over 10,000 people directly as it conducts research relating to the disabled, retarded, and disadvantaged.

Henry Viscardi was appointed by President Ford to serve as chairman of the White House Conference on Handicapped Individuals, and this appointment has been continued by President Carter.

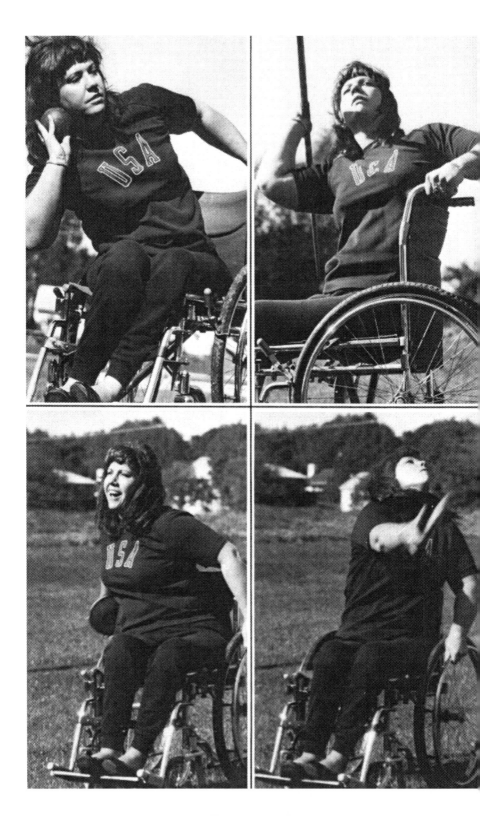

THE NINETEEN SIXTIES

For the physically disabled, life was expanding in the sixties, though growth sometimes alternated with frustration outside the world of wheelchair sports. New vocational rehabilitation amendments were passed. New rehabilitation centers were constructed. Grants were issued to speed up improvements in workshops for the disabled. Economic need was eliminated as a requirement for obtaining rehabilitation services, and the National Commission on Architectural Barriers was formed. Support increased for a National Center for the Deaf, Blind-Youth and Adults, and a special program for disabled migrants was organized. The sixties also gave birth to a new federal government agency, the Social and Rehabilitation Service. An umbrella

Superstar Rosalie Hixson, post-polio, tossing shot (top left), *throwing the javelin* (top right), *and throwing the discus* (bottom). *(Photo 1976)*

agency, its purpose was to bring about better coordination in the provision of services for a broad range of vulnerable citizens of this country, such as the aged, the handicapped, and those in need of financial assistance.

Though improvements were happening, they weren't happening fast enough. Rehabilitation brought thousands of the disabled to the point where they could take care of themselves in most cases and lead relatively independent lives. But there were problems of education, employment, housing, and architectural barriers. The disabled asked in angry frustration what good was it to be rehabilitated if there was no road leading ahead from that point. The hiring habits of employers had not changed drastically. Schools were inadequately prepared for the physically disabled student; most of the time the student was segregated in a "special school." And everywhere, even in new buildings where architects should have been aware of the growing need for accessibility, there were still steps and narrow doorways.

The disabled, once passive, once unsure, were starting to become persistent about their needs and their rights. They were beginning to ask questions of themselves and others: "Is it not our right to be fairly interviewed for a job, and if we qualify, to be hired?" "Is it not our right to travel on an airplane, train, bus?" "Are we any less individuals or citizens of this country because we cannot use our legs and because we are physically disabled?"

Out of this combustible mood, and determination to prove once and for all the ability of the disabled, emerged a new element in wheelchair sports—the superstar.

A star is one who is a leading performer. A superstar is one who goes beyond the expected into the zone of the untried and the unknown. Alonzo Wilkins, in the fifties, had shown the way. Those in wheelchair sports knew it would happen. They didn't know when, but the sixties brought moments of expectation, while superstars developed slowly throughout the land. Time, endurance, determination, perseverance, the desire to be tested, the strength to go beyond what already existed, were part of the personality of the superior athlete.

A player on the field during one of the Regionals was trying to explain the ingredients that go into a superstar. At one time he himself had been a superstar in able-bodied sports, so he recognized and respected the quality in others. "This kid comes out on the field," he said, "and tosses the javelin and breaks my old record. Well, I hadn't been training much, but I took a stab at it and broke his record. And then it was his last shot. He turned and looked at me, and I saw it in his eyes. Clear as anything, the look of pure fierce determination to win. He threw the javelin; he broke my record; and some day he's going to be up there with the superstars."

Perhaps the moment of stardom comes after there has been a loss, when others would retreat or give up. Athletes who go on at this point sometimes pull strength from resources they never knew they had. Superstars refer to the "down" times in their lives, times when they weren't getting it together, when their records were in danger of being broken. It is during these times—against the odds, in spite of the pressures—that such athletes draw deep down inside themselves, reach for the rush that would push them past the peak.

Bill Johnson is one of those superstars. Bill was on the first team in 1960 to represent the United States in the Paralympics. In 1960, there were four hundred paraplegics representing twenty-two nations at the first Paralympics in Rome. (Every fourth year from 1960 on, the Paralympics would be held in the same city that was host to the regular Olympics.) Bill and the other veterans who traveled to Europe went this time not in war but in peace. They were the first ambassadors to represent wheelchair sports from this country.

Bill, one of the earlier members of the Flying Wheels Championship Basketball Team, came from Long Beach, California. He was twenty-two when he became disabled. He had enlisted in the Korean War. At the air-force base, Bill showed his skill in baseball and basketball. One day he was hitching a ride back to his base near East St. Louis. There was an automobile accident. The next day, the 6-foot 2-inch athlete was physically disabled.

Bill remembers doctors asking him what he liked to do before he was injured. All he could think of was that he had loved sports. So he joined the Flying Wheels while he was in the hospital in California, and in his very first year of competition became a member of the third All-American basketball team. Bill made three cross-country tours with the Long Beach Flying Wheels. His blue eyes light up with enthusiasm as he talks of those tours. The objective was to go to all the different VA hospitals, to play before the patients, and to increase the number of wheelchair players—at that time estimated to be two hundred. The team traveled to the Great Lakes Naval Station, to Walter Reed Hospital in Bethesda, Maryland, and to St. Albans Veterans Hospital in New York, free of charge, just to make the public and the newly disabled veterans aware.

As a wheelchair basketball player, Bill received the All-American Award six times and was named most valuable player four times. His opponents grew to dread his unerring two-hand set shots. After winning the Helms Athletic Award, the blond veteran found himself a member of that first United States team traveling to the Paralympics. (Those selected for the international team were chosen mainly on the basis of achievement at the National Wheelchair Games, and with expectation as to how well they would perform internationally.)

The Olympic Center in Rome was built atop a flight of stairs, which had to be climbed in order to get to the village. Many of the disabled shuddered when they saw those stairs. No one had taken into consideration the fact that the athletes would be in wheelchairs, and that the steps would make the center inaccessible. It was the first time that Rome had been exposed to such a situation. And it was also the first time for the United States and for athletes such as Bill Johnson. They realized they would have to learn together as wheelchair sports spread throughout the world. So they were all carried up the stairs to the Olympic Center.

Through participating in several Paralympics, Bill got the chance to travel all over the world. He remembers vividly putting on a demonstration in downtown Hong

Kong in a makeshift gym. Feelings against Americans were high at that time. Some small, poorly dressed children were standing, peeking through the screens. They looked hungry. When sandwiches were served, Bill offered them to the children. He can recall the hurt he felt when they threw the sandwiches on the floor in front of him. In sports, it had been easy to forget such hatred existed.

In Hong Kong and in many countries that Bill visited, the disabled were practically invisible, rarely seen on the streets. In Japan, during one basketball exhibition, the disabled were brought in from a sanitarium far out in the country. The basketball players were tied in their chairs, and it was clear that the team had barely been "rehabilitated" in time for the games. The players kept tipping over, and it was a game that the sensitive Bill Johnson prefers to forget.

During his years of competition, Bill captured many first, second, and third places in both backstroke and breaststroke. A national table-tennis champion, ranked second in the 50-meter backstroke and the javelin throw, Bill is now player-coach with the Long Beach Flying Wheels Basketball Team, the same team with which he started. Four of the original five members of the Flying Wheels have since died. Bill now fills his line with veterans from the Vietnam War as he tries to keep his team going.

He has also coached in the Lakewood Recreation Department, where his able-bodied boys' team established a 39-9 baseball record and won a league championship.

Bill has done some professional acting, but he minimizes his movie roles. "They were just small parts," he says. He appeared in the *Roy Campanella Story* and in *The Other Side of the Mountain,* the life story of Jill Kinmont.

He loves wheelchair sports. He still shows up at competitions, and the other athletes are aware of his presence. To Bill, wheelchair sports mean comradeship, a feeling that grows stronger as the years go on.

Nineteen sixty-one, the year after Bill's first appearance in the Paralympics, brought another superstar to the games: Stefan Florescu, a quadriplegic from Michigan.

Stef is a Romanian, fluent in several languages, whose parents emigrated to the United States. His father, a tailor, and his mother settled with their three boys in Davenport, Iowa.

Stef learned at an early age what a language barrier can do. During his boyhood, his mother still spoke only her native tongue, and the ways of America were very new to her. She worried about Stef's having a sufficient supply of drinking water in school, since, in Romania, the school did not supply water for students. Finding some beautiful whiskey bottles and not knowing what sort of bottles they were, she decided to fill a different one for Stef each day with water. And each day Stef religiously took his new whiskey bottle filled with water to school, neither caring about nor understanding the jeers of his classmates. Stef is still that kind of person, strong-minded, not too disturbed by what other people may think.

In the late forties, Stef was a member of his St. Ambrose College track team and received the outstanding track athlete award. A four-letter winner, he transferred his energies and talent to intramural table tennis and basketball.

Then his world seemed to split apart. He took a dive off the shallow end of a dock at a lake near Flint, Michigan. He came out of his accident a quadriplegic. Stef's parents, filled with love and devotion, moved across the street from the hospital that Stef would call his home for two years.

When he was finally discharged, he found himself viewing life from a set of wheels. It meant a drastic change in his means of locomotion. But his love for sports did not change, nor did his feeling of being an individual.

Mrs. Connie Curto, an employee of the YWCA and a pioneer in the teaching of synchronized swimming in the Detroit area, encouraged and coached Stef in using the limited motion in his arms to swim. He swam for several years at Detroit's Patton Swimming Pool under the supervision of swimming director James D. Moore. When Robert Classon, a former president of the Paralyzed Veterans of America, urged him to attend the fifth National Wheelchair Games in 1961, Stef was eager. His long love of sports came to life at those games. Founder Benjamin Lipton and his committee were impressed with his performance.

Stef went back home to organize the Michigan Paralyzed Veterans of America and the Rolling Romanians' wheelchair track team. He also coached the National Association of the Physically Handicapped (NAPH) women's team.

Stef became the first United States team member to win a gold medal in table tennis in international competition.

He found through his competing that training for the meets was an excellent way to maintain his health. As part of his continuous rehabilitation and training schedule, Stef would push himself around the neighborhood from a half to two miles daily.

One of the strongest memories of competition that Stef carries with him is the time a young twenty-year-old man from Norway, whose last name was Esplund, competed with him in the quad table-tennis singles. Stef couldn't figure out how Esplund was going to compete since he apparently couldn't move his arms or hands at all. Stef was eliminated in the quarter finals by a young Englishman. Esplund beat the Englishman by using only his neck and head during the final match. He held the paddle between his teeth.

Stef's able-bodied wife is the former Caroline Tupper, a graduate of St. Thomas Aquinas College and a lawyer. She is a faithful follower of wheelchair sports, and her enthusiasm is constant as she accompanies Stef on his travels. The Rolling Romanian and his wife are a familiar sight as he wheels across the field from one competition to another.

Stef's belief in what quads can accomplish opened up new doors in wheelchair sports. It also earned him the first award ever received by a quadriplegic or a paraplegic for completing the Red Cross 50-mile swim.

Women began to compete nationally in wheelchair sports in 1962, and became a permanent part of the competitions in 1963. Women produced superstars of their own.

It took Evelyn Moore, a quadriplegic, almost a year before she could swim the length of a pool. Yet she made it to the New York Nationals in 1963, when there was just a handful of women.

Evelyn, a social worker, became disabled as the result of an automobile accident. She was at the New York Institute of Physical Medicine and Rehabilitation for eleven-and-a-half months. There were many people pulling for her, remembering her during her long stay in the hospital. Evelyn's mother worked full-time, yet she drove forty miles each day during those months to visit her daughter and to keep her spirits up. Evelyn's father, brother, and sister gave her constant support.

Her first try at the Nationals was a big disappointment. Even though she won her table-tennis match and was supposed to return to play another match, Evelyn didn't go back. She felt out of place. All the other participants seemed to be having such a good time. They didn't appear to be as handicapped as she felt she was as a quadriplegic. Evelyn didn't approach anyone to make friends. Not being outgoing, she kept to herself and left the Nationals thinking she would not attend again.

Many disabled competitors feel that way the first time around. Everyone seems to belong to a group. Old friends get together and share memories. The new athletes are awed and sometimes frightened by the skill on the field. The first year a new wheelchair sports athlete has really time only to see what it's all about, to digest it, to begin, to reach out—for the new friendship, and to start one's own share of memories.

Evelyn's brother Phil and her mother faithfully took her

to a weekly handicapped swimming class for a year before she entered the University of Illinois.

Evelyn's life took an upward sweep when she started her courses at the university. Until then she had been dependent on others for pushing her, dressing her, and taking care of her physical needs. But Tim Nugent and his rehabilitation staff, as he had done with so many others before Evelyn, took her in hand. Within six months she was totally independent. At the university she saw people with the same disability functioning independently. She realized it could be done. There was no one around to pamper her. At home and in the hospital, there were always a diligent mother and well-meaning nurses and therapists to help her over the rough moments. At Illinois, Evelyn found that she could handle the rough moments herself. Her independence came from trying and trying over and over again. She left the university with a B.A. in sociology.

Evelyn Moore went back to the Nationals in 1964, and placed second in back freestyle, first in bowling, and first in table tennis. The girl who felt alone and frightened at her first Nationals in New York, went on to Tokyo in 1964 to win a gold medal for front freestyle and a gold medal for the backstroke.

In her Class 1A competition she has proven to be the consistently best competitor in the country and has been accepted on most of the international teams in the years she competed.

In 1960, the disabled athlete not only had to struggle to train to compete on the field. He was involved in daily struggles off the field. There were the times when teams had to search for new places to practice because the gyms were reserved for able-bodied competitions. There was a lack of money. It cost money to belong to the basketball league, to travel, to reach the Regionals and Nationals. There were equipment expenses. It meant wheelchair athletes had to depend on contributions.

Ben Lipton did as much as he could to help disabled competitors reach the games. The United States team's trip to the international games was arranged and financed through his efforts, through the cooperation of interested individuals, organizations, teams, and by the participants themselves. Everyone pitched in but still there was never quite enough; there was always a last-minute hustle and a chance that the money wouldn't be there and the trip couldn't be made.

To help insure the wheelchair athletes against inadequate funds, Ben Lipton incorporated and organized the United States Wheelchair Sports Fund in 1961. The Sports Fund continued through the years with its goals to foster goodwill and understanding between the United States and other countries through international wheelchair sports activities, and to promote the growth of wheelchair sports and recreation in the United States. But the Sports Fund's largest annual project was support for the United States wheelchair team that went to the Paralympics.

Another area of support came from the Triffid Bowmen, an archery club dedicated to furthering the growth of that sport and assisting people in need. The club supported the

National Wheelchair Games for many years as officials, and as judges of the archery competitions. The Bowmen Archers also involved themselves in training and coaching wheelchair archers and in fund-raising.

Surmounting the obstacles, superstar after superstar found their way to the Nationals in the sixties. The word was out. At last there was a place for the serious disabled athlete to compete. In spite of the financial frustrations and growing pains of wheelchair sports, each event would eventually gather its share of heroes who would annually set, break, and reset their own records. It was archery's turn in the sixties, and it came in the person of Jack Whitman.

Jack grew up on a farm. His parents were grain and livestock farmers in Central Illinois. From the age of seven he spent many hours working in the fields; by the time he was ten, he was driving a tractor and working some days from sunrise to sunset. Jack Whitman learned about hard work, and his young body grew powerful from throwing 80-pound bales of hay over his head. The years spent scooping grain, juggling bales, traveling on horses with his grandfather over the 240-acre farm were good years. They helped build the supply of physical endurance that Jack would use later to become one of the top wheelchair archers in the world.

Jack had a football scholarship at the University of Illinois. He was a physical education major. In his freshman year at college, he became a member of both the football and baseball teams.

When he was a sophomore, Jack fell from a piece of

gymnasium equipment and broke his neck. At nineteen, as a quadriplegic, he accepted the fact that his life, the exhilarating dashing life of the star athlete, was over.

Before the accident, his philosophy had always been to live each day, each minute, as it came. He also believed that if you want to amount to something, you have to work to earn it.

He thought a lot about that philosophy while he lay on his back. He decided to work with what he had, applying the same principles to his new situation and to new goals.

Jack began his new approach by enrolling in the rehabilitation program for handicapped persons at the university. By chance, a neighbor of Jack's parents sent him a straight wooden bow. That bow would lead him to capture national and international fame in archery and leave a history of one broken archery record after another.

As a champion, Jack had two distinct careers in archery. Between the years 1960 and 1965, he had the benefit of being coached by the members of the Champaign Urbana Osage Archery Club. During those years of training and competition, he found most of his hours occupied by the bow and target. Because competitors in wheelchairs often begin with weak arms or poor balance, he found he had to work much harder than a standing archer to get a high score.

Jack competed in about thirty-five weekend tournaments a year. The meets varied from club, regional, state and international competition. He put in forty to forty-five hours a week of practice for the tournaments. Jack would shoot after work, sometimes more than five hours a day, and Saturday and Sunday would find him shooting ten hours a day. It was a grueling schedule forty-eight weeks a year, but he had the endurance of a young farmer and the training routine of a champion. During his vigorous training program, Jack gave up practically everything but shooting a bow, working, and sleeping. It was a difficult style of living for his young wife, Jan, one that required much understanding and unselfishness on her part.

Jack immediately qualified on his first trip to the Nationals and was chosen to travel to the first Paralympics. In Rome, he won his first gold medal on his thirtieth birthday.

Jack Whitman remained undefeated in both national and international competition until the 1964 Paralympics in Japan. He held the record for every round in wheelchair archery in which he competed. In 1962, he set the record for the newly introduced American Round in the National Wheelchair Games.

The next year he came away from the International Stoke-Mandeville Games as the International Wheelchair Archery Champion, setting two international records.

In the mid sixties, Jack turned to coaching. An arthritic condition and shoulder surgery forced his retirement from competition. But even though he had hung up his bow as a competitor, he would turn to teaching others to raise their bows and shoot with excellence.

Jack developed a booklet called *Coaching Techniques for Wheelchair Archery*. His archery students have won about twenty-three individual championships in national games competition since 1967, and several international championships. Five of the six records maintained by the National Wheelchair Archery Association have been held by his students.

It's easy to spot Jack's students on the archery range, with their style, their graceful follow-up, their dedicated respect for the sport. And usually at the competitions is their concerned coach, wearing the orange and blue colors of the University of Illinois, his green eyes wandering over the line of archers, checking on his crew, beaming at their accomplishments, rejoicing with them in their victories—a superstar in whatever capacity he operates.

It was in the early sixties that the American Wheelchair Bowling Association (AWBA) was formed. Wheelchair bowling soon became a part of the Nationals.

Avid bowlers poured into New York. Paraplegics awed the audiences with their power, quadriplegics with their ingenuity.

Many of the quads used stick bowling: with a shuffle-boardlike stick they pushed the ball down the alley. Some used a ball with a spring-loaded handle that snapped back into the ball after delivery. Both of these variations were allowed in national competition because they both required the bowler to aim and deliver the ball. Because the quadriplegic's arm and hand strength were limited, new techniques and devices were constantly being developed to bring more excitement to bowling.

For those who had limited muscle power, the invention of the chute made bowling possible. (Chute bowling was not allowed in national competition because it was not motivated and directed by the bowler.) The chute was built so that a wheelchair could roll up on it and the bowler need only push the ball down the ramp for delivery. Many would be able to enjoy the recreation benefits of bowling through the invention of the chute.

John Ebert, originally from Long Island, left his mark as one of the most exciting quadriplegic bowlers ever to come to the tournaments. A competitor for sixteen years, John five times won first place in the quadriplegic class at the National Wheelchair Games. Though a quadriplegic, with limited arm power, John did not use any of the adaptive-device styles of bowling.

A gold-medal winner in table tennis, John managed the Eastern PVA (Paralyzed Veterans of America) basketball and track teams and the Fort Lauderdale Gold Coasters wheelchair basketball team. He once bowled a single game with total pins of 199.

Eventually the abundance of bowlers, both paras (paraplegics) and quads, and the time it took to compete, became too much for the Nationals to handle. Bowling was a time-consuming sport, and the days were already crammed with hourly events and too little time in which to compete. Bowling was dropped from the Nationals. Tournaments through the AWBA are still held throughout the country, and there is a yearly July national tournament in which top bowlers compete.

Two superstars would crest the horizon and emerge in the 1964 Paralympics in Tokyo, Japan—one, a former diver; the other, a farm girl.

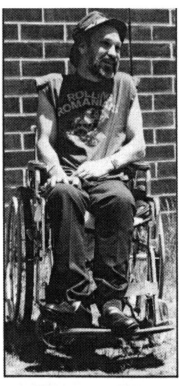

Top left: *Quadriplegic Stefan Florescu, who opened up wheelchair competition for "quads."* Top right: *Coach Jack Whitman, a quadriplegic. (Both photographs from the Twentieth National Wheelchair Athletic Games, Farmingdale, New York, 1976).*

From left to right: *Archers Russell Stone, a double amputee, Bill Myers, a paraplegic, and Olaf Hurd, paraplegic, practicing at the Woodrow Wilson Rehabilitation Center, Fisherville, Virginia, 1976.*

Weight lifter Eddie Coyle, post-polio: National, World, Pan Am, and Para-lympic Weightlifting Champion.

The women's 60-yard dash at the National Wheelchair Athletic Games, 1976; at left, *Darlene Quinlan, a paraplegic.*

Competition for places on the 1964 United States Paralympic team was intense. The entrants now had training programs, which put them in excellent shape for the trials. George Conn took his place on the team by placing first in freestyle, breaststroke, and backstroke in Class II swimming. He broke all records previously held, including setting one of his own—51.1 seconds for the 50-yard breaststroke.

George had been injured as a result of an automobile accident while on active duty with the United States Air Force at Scott Air Force Base, near St. Louis. Before his injury, he had been a diver at Northwestern University. He credits his diving experience with saving his life: when he was thrown 250 feet from the automobile, he was able to control his body attitude during his downward plunge. He feels this saved him from more serious injuries.

George was in the hospital for fourteen months and was retired by the air force. He spent those hospital months thinking of how he could remain in the sports he loved, and again develop the skills he had once had. When he got out of the hospital, he enrolled in night school. But his days were spent exercising, getting his body ready.

George, a paraplegic, began his competition in wheelchair sports with the Gizz Kids of Illinois, and he concentrated on swimming and basketball.

He was soon selected to be a member of a wheelchair athletic demonstration team from Illinois, which was to tour South Africa, Rhodesia, and Zambia. The team consisted of fourteen men, four women, and six escorts. In the summer of 1962, following the National Wheelchair Games in New York, George and the United States team flew to London where they began their tour. They traveled by aircraft and van, covering approximately twenty-five cities and five thousand miles, and they gave at least two demonstrations a day in each locale. One demonstration was before twelve hundred Bantu paraplegics at the Rhudeport Durban Mine Hospital, outside Johannesburg, where they put together the first integrated sports event held in South Africa since 1948. George would never forget the time they played basketball at Kitwe in the far northern reaches of the copper country. Fifty women of a local tribe attended the game. The team played the game on a court constructed of oiled sand. By half time, George and his team members had hands that were raw.

When George Conn went to Japan for the Paralympics in 1964, he and the other competitors were delighted and relieved to find ramps leading the way to the Olympic Village in Tokyo.

During his Paralympic career, George played twenty-seven consecutive international basketball games and was never on a losing team. In the National Wheelchair Games, in swimming competition, he won eleven gold medals and one silver, and set and consecutively broke eleven National Games records. In the International Paralympic swimming competition, he won seventeen of a possible twenty gold medals and set eight world records. The United States team came back from the Paralympics in Japan with fifty gold, forty-four silver, and thirty-one bronze medals. There were sixty-six competitors; each one contributed to the splendid accomplishments of the United States team.

Something else happened at those Tokyo games that

would change the history of wheelchair sports. It was there in Japan that a young American girl named Rosalie Hixson became the champion woman wheelchair athlete.

Rosie came from a farm in Crystal Springs, Pennsylvania. There her days had been filled with feeding the chickens, milking the cows, helping with the plowing. Her parents raised beef cattle. The Hixson family lived in an old farmhouse high atop a hill overlooking the valley. There were about three hundred acres on which to run free with her brother and three sisters.

Rosie had her own private corner of that farm, her own circle of a world. It was where she tended her vegetable garden, and it was where she dared to dream of becoming an Olympic star—a broad jumper on an Olympic team, traveling across the ocean, throughout the world.

In between driving the tractor, loading the hay, Rosie practiced for her dream. She'd use the time coming home from school running, jumping fences, doing anything to strengthen her legs and increase her speed. She did all the things she thought broad jumpers must do in order to become the best.

In between broad jumping and the farm, there were the quiet times of reading every sort of book about horses and nature. There were the wintertimes of ice skating, and spine-tingling rides on the big bobsled, which seated fifteen, had a steering wheel, and was pulled behind the tractor up the hills. There were the joyful times when the entire family would gather around the piano and fill the long winter nights with singing.

It was on Halloween when Rosie was just turning

fifteen that she was struck down by polio and became a paraplegic. Rosie's parents, her family, were devastated by the news, but Rosie, unable yet to comprehend the change her life had taken, felt only a strange excitement. A classmate whom she admired was in a wheelchair, and it seemed to her that being in the same category as he was assured her definitely of an honorable position. If she could turn out the way he had, everything would be fine. During her year in the hospital, however, Rosie began to experience those moments of depression familiar to the newly disabled. She missed her freedom. She missed the farm and the Olympics dream she had carried for so long.

A therapist at Elizabethtown influenced Rosie's thinking. One day she sat down with Rosie and told her, This is the way it is, this is the way it's going to be. It was at that moment that Rosie faced the whole meaning of never being able to walk again.

Rosie went back to school and graduated with her class. The farm was a different place for her when she returned. She knew there were still things she had to adjust to, things she must learn about her new situation.

Part of that adjustment and learning came at the Johnstown (Pennsylvania) Rehabilitation Center. There she met Lou Neishloss, a recreation instructor, who introduced her to wheelchair sports.

Lou was involved as coach of the men's wheelchair track and field and basketball teams. In three days he taught Rosie to swim. It was during those swimming sessions that Rosie felt her life was being given back to her.

Lou encouraged her to join the wheelchair sports team at

the center. The days that followed were strenuous ones for Rosie, working out six and eight hours a day, with special diets, weight training, exercises, actually practicing for the different events.

Rosie took out her dream again. She heard of the Paralympics. She knew of the great wheelchair athletes traveling around the world. She felt she had been led to this point of time in her life. Someday she would be one of them. She didn't know then that she was also on her way to becoming the champion woman wheelchair athlete of the world.

As a member of the BVR (Bureau of Vocational Rehabilitation) Wheelers of the Johnstown Rehabilitation Center, Rosie stunned the audience with her great athletic ability. Later she would help form the Central Penn Wheelers Sports Team.

The five-foot nine-inch girl kept returning from the Nationals and Paralympics loaded down with medals. In one year's competition alone, she won seventeen first places, nine seconds, and three thirds. She was named outstanding athlete of the first Pan American Games in Winnipeg, Canada, with a 63-point contribution to the United States total. She earned nine gold medals, including three in swimming.

In Tokyo, the girl who came from the farm in Crystal Springs, Pennsylvania, captured first place and topped the American field with six gold and two silver medals. She won first place in the javelin, discus, club throws, shot put, the freestyle and backstroke swimming events, establishing herself as the greatest woman athlete ever to compete in the

Paralympics. Rosie came in second in the precision, the javelin, and the breaststroke. Rosie Hixson, first woman on a United States team to complete the physical fitness swim of fifty miles, held her audience spellbound with her versatility. Rosie often competed in as many as eighteen events, when competition such as this was unlimited.

Rosie has a thing about freedom. Perhaps it comes from the time on the farm; perhaps the farm left that with her. She doesn't like to be tied down. Rosie moves around a lot, likes photography, cooking, riding motorcycles, speed, and always a touch of danger.

Tell Rosie Hixson she can't win and those catlike hazel eyes light up with the challenge. Yet there is a shyness about her that actually caused her to hide at an international competition when she was to be presented with her medals.

Each competitor comes home with a memory tucked inside that she or he knows will remain forever. Rosie captured such a memory at the Paralympics held in Heidelberg, Germany, in 1972. She had completed the competitions with her record in the javelin still good. With bronze and silver medals hanging around her neck, she carried with her the memory of that beautiful night in Heidelberg, Germany, when the town put on a fireworks display. There in the sky, brilliant in color, were the Paralympics wheels lighting the night. Looking up and seeing those wheels in the sky was just part of the magic that wheelchair sports had brought to Rosie. The rest of the magic had come from Rosie herself and a dream that wouldn't die.

In the sixties, wheelchair athletes like Rosie were beginning to gather public recognition. There were friends and family at the airport now, eager faces waiting to hear about the exciting adventures in far-off lands.

A new area of competition opened up in 1967 with the Pan Am Games. The Pan American competitions included athletes from North, Central, and South America. The games were held in Winnipeg, Canada, in 1967; Buenos Aires, Argentina, in 1969; Kingston, Jamaica, in 1971; Lima, Peru, in 1973; and Mexico City, Mexico, in 1975. Soon afterward the Pan Am Council was organized to provide for competition every two years in the countries of North and South America and to develop in all the countries of both continents participation in wheelchair sports.

As the world became more involved in wheelchair sports, so did the methods of participating in the sport. The racing wheelchair had become popular. The official sports chair had pneumatic tires (better than hard rubber for daily use as well as sports) with wheels 24 inches in diameter. The seat of the chair could not be higher than 21 inches from the ground. A larger wheel would give the athlete a special advantage in the dashes. A higher seat would give him the advantage in field events. New rules were designed around the sports wheelchair. A strap would have to be attached firmly and drawn reasonably taut between the telescopic bars extending to the footrest platforms. This was a safety feature. A paralyzed leg might fall off the foot platform and land on the surface and become injured. It was also a fair-play feature, in that a nonparalyzed leg might intentionally or automatically slip off the platform and serve as an emergency steering device in dashes or stability control in field events.

The foot platform itself was set at 4⅞ inches from the ground to the leading edge for purely safety reasons. This height was found best for the chair's stability. Should it be any lower, it tended to bind on a playing surface; should it be higher, the center of balance of the chair was dangerously moved to the rear.

The rules and regulations multiplied, and so did the players. As early as 1965, Stef Florescu of Michigan had been experimenting with Regionals in his area. After attending the Nationals himself, Stef had become convinced that wheelchair sports needed regional meets as a preliminary to the Nationals and also as an additional incentive for state or regional championships. Stef had talked the Detroit Department of Parks and Recreation into getting him practice areas and a staff to help him with the running of the Regional Michigan Meet.

Stef's Regional was held in May 1965 before the National Wheelchair Athletic Committee had spelled out guidelines for organizing the games, but it acted as a stimulus for others to follow.

Along came Charlie Ryder of Pennsylvania. Charlie, who had been with Ben Lipton at the beginning at Adelphi University, was trying out a Pennsylvania Regional in his area. The Pennsylvania Regional held in May 1968 gave competitors the chance to match their skills at a meet other than the National.

Charlie was a familiar figure during the Regionals,

perspiring under the blistering spring sun, his walkie-talkie in hand, communicating with field coaches and officials, running constantly back and forth across the field. He supervised everything, from every event throughout the weekend to the lunches and the final banquet when the competitions were done. There were always people to thank, new champions to congratulate, and Charlie always remembered each and every person who was involved. Over sixty-five athletes showed up for Charlie Ryder's exciting mininational. Everyone in wheelchair sports watched and waited, wondering if the regional competition that had begun in Michigan and was now moving slowly through Pennsylvania would catch on.

With the expansion of opportunities for competitions, the classification of wheelchair athletes would become more complicated and far more imperative. New teams were springing up around the country. With more disabled entering competitions, there was more variety in disabilities. Officials found that a refined classification was urgent.

Dr. Caibre McCann was in charge of classifying the athletes for the events. For this very intense and tricky procedure, which could cause serious repercussions if incorrectly done, the rules have been amended somewhat from year to year. But the main structure remains the same.

The system of classifying is based on the concept of different levels of disability related to the spinal cord. A spinal-cord injury at the neck means a severe disability—the higher the injury, the more parts are involved. If there is an injury at the neck, everything below, including the arms and legs, is paralyzed. A lower-level injury in the low-back portion of the spinal cord is defined as a lesser degree of disability. A doctor's accurate classification of a disabled athlete is crucial to that athlete's performance in competition. A paraplegic with excellent balance and strong back and stomach muscles would certainly have an advantage over a paraplegic with little or no balance. A quadriplegic with some arm movement, throwing the javelin, could never fairly compete with a quadriplegic with no arm movement.

It was onward and upward for the United States Paralympic Team now. In 1968, they traveled to Israel. Superstar Darlene Quinlan was one of the athletes who qualified for the trip.

Darlene, who had been disabled in an automobile accident at the age of eight, started competing in wheelchair sports as a paraplegic when she was sixteen. It was through the help of Karen Johnstone, a physical therapist at a rehabilitation center, that Darlene became interested in the competitive aspect of swimming. Karen is still Darlene's coach today.

Besides the backstroke and freestyle, Karen coached her in discus, javelin, shot put, 60-yard dash, and later in precision javelin and slalom.

During her first trip to the National Wheelchair Games in New York, Darlene set two National Games records— one in discus and one in shot put. She won her first gold medal in the backstroke at the Israel Internationals. With seven hundred competitors challenging some of the records, there was a surge of pressure on all the athletes. But Darlene thrived on that pressure.

She brought back memories of the trip that would never fade: a lifetime picture of the Sea of Galilee, the buses with collapsible ramps, the great sports center in Ramat Gan, founded and run by the Israel Foundation for Handicapped Children (ILAN). The state of Israel was excitingly rehabilitation-minded. Israel is probably the only country in the world where the constitution provides for the unrestricted immigration of the sick and disabled. The most chronically disabled immigrant could come and settle in Israel and become a citizen, eligible for full rehabilitation. Perhaps that country's own experience with war and with horrifying disability has led to its understanding and ability to cope with all disabled.

Darlene was there at the opening ceremonies in the new University of Jerusalem stadium when all the teams paraded in rows of threes around the field behind the bands. She thrilled to the standing ovation the United States team received when it entered the stadium.

Darlene and her teammates appreciated the conveniences provided by the Israelis, such as the temporary toilets with collapsible canvas partitions. In many countries, bathroom and personal-care facilities were so poor that the disabled were often left without accommodations and had to provide their own.

Six hundred members of the high school premilitary training corps were given special leave to serve with the games. These high school students acted as runners, ushers, wheelchair pushers, equipment retrievers, and personal messengers. The warmth, the smiling faces of the young helpers, the roar of the fifteen thousand in the stadium audience that welcomed the teams, symbolized the essence, the core of wheelchair sports.

After her stay in Israel, Darlene traveled (on tour) with the team to Rome, where she had a private audience with the Pope, and to Greece.

Darlene, who is never happy unless she throws as far as she can or pushes as fast as she knows she is able, was a member of the Detroit Sparks and then joined the Motor City Wheelers, a wheelchair sports team.

She played on women's wheelchair basketball teams in Michigan and helped organize a women's open tournament in Detroit. Her team—the Detroit Ball Bearings—took first place, and Darlene was selected one of five players for the All-Star Team.

Darlene trains eight months a year, from January until April for track and field and from April until August for basketball. She holds three records in Michigan for discus, shot put and javelin, and four national records in discus, javelin, shot put and 60-yard dash. She also holds an international javelin record. Each year since 1968, Darlene has qualified as a member of the United States international wheelchair team. Recently honored as Sportswoman of the Year at a United Fund Torch Drive in Detroit, Michigan, and elected to the National Wheelchair Sports Hall of Fame, she is also involved behind the scene in wheelchair sports as board member of the Michigan Wheelchair Athletic Conference.

A lovely, striking-looking girl, dark eyes deep with

concentration, a headband gathering her full dark hair away from her face, Darlene can be seen sitting under a tree on the field, watching the competitors ahead of her, measuring what threat they may be, as though she and her competition were the only ones on the field. Intense, serious, dedicated, unable to stop at second best, almost driven to go past what is expected, Darlene is typical of the superstar who came out of the sixties.

Though superstars invaded the sixties, wheelchair sports existed not only because of the extraordinary athlete, but because of the hundreds and even thousands of athletes around the country who were joining the events, coming out and bringing others with them, contributing their skills, showing that the disabled could travel, could toss a javelin, that a "quad" could throw a club. Each athlete who would join wheelchair sports, in whatever capacity, with whatever talents he might reach for, was part of an educational process to enlighten the able-bodied as to the ability of the disabled. All athletes, those who succeeded, those who failed to qualify for the Nationals, those who competed in the Regionals and went away without breaking a record, still established a heroic mark in history as they dared to show it could be done.

The Disabled and the Bill of Rights

Illinois was the first state to include in its constitution an article guaranteeing equal opportunity in employment, housing, education, and access to places of public accommodation to handicapped persons. This move which took place in 1972 served as an example to the many states that lacked legislation for the disabled.

Iowa, Wisconsin, New Jersey, New York, and Alaska soon followed, passing civil rights legislation for the handicapped. An example of an amendment passed by Iowa prohibiting discrimination against the handicapped reads as follows:

"Disability" means the physical or mental condition of a person which constitutes a substantial handicap. In reference to employment, under this chapter, "disability" also means the physical or mental condition of a person which constitutes a substantial handicap, but is unrelated to such person's ability to engage in a particular occupation.

The amendment touches labor organizations, housing, and employment agencies. Although legally worded, its intent quite simply is to include the disabled in society, incorporating them into life.

State after state is gradually passing legislation prohibiting discrimination against the handicapped, thereby insuring equal opportunity and basic human dignity to all citizens.

The National Association of the Physically Handicapped, Inc., adopted their own Bill of Rights in July 1964 in Detroit, Michigan. The bill and resolutions formed at the convention affected millions of disabled in this country. The bill claims rights for the disabled as follows:

The right to the earliest possible diagnosis and treatment for disabilities or injuries to aid in achieving a maximum recovery.

The right to an adequate public education.

The right to an adequate training or retraining for a vocation in which the individual's physical capacities and his aptitudes can be most productive and in which the individual finds satisfaction.

The right to equal pay for equal work.

The right to the elimination of architectural barriers to provide an accessible entrance to public buildings, spiritual, educational, cultural and recreational buildings and other areas, such as parks, campsites, beaches, and marinas, used by the general public as a place of gathering or amusement, so that the physically handicapped may discharge their duties as citizens and fulfill their desires socially. (1967: Passage of Architectural Facilities Act eliminating architectural barriers.)

The right to use public transportation (air, buses, rapid transit, trains) through the development of barrier-free design conveyances.

The right to purchase life, accident, and hospitalization (health) insurance at normal rates.

The right to purchase automobile insurance at normal rates unless the driver has proven to be a bad risk.

The right to housing and custodial care that meets lawful standards and includes opportunities to exercise one's intellect.

The right to accessible facilities in the area of civil defense.

The right to proper legal safeguards.

The right to have physically handicapped persons and the organized physically handicapped as participants in any group making decisions affecting their lives.

Either a comprehensive civil rights bill written into state constitutions or the Bill of Rights created by NAPH, if carried out to any degree, will certainly improve life for the 44,000,000 handicapped children and adults in the United States. More than 1,500,000 are epileptics; more than 435,000 people are totally or partially blind; more than 236,000 are deaf; more than 2,000,000 have some hearing loss; more than 750,000 have cerebral palsy; multiple sclerosis claims 260,000; muscular dystrophy victims number more than 200,000. The mentally retarded number more than 6,000,000. Annually, 440,000 new cases of stroke are diagnosed. One in every eleven adults is estimated to be severely disabled.

How do people feel about the physically disabled population? Jerome Siller, professor of educational psychology at New York University, took a survey on the feelings of some 400 men and women toward people who were affected with certain disabilities.

Of the eight disabilities mentioned, blindness and deafness were the most socially acceptable, because visually they caused less distress than physical deformity. Cerebral palsy and physical deformity ranked the least acceptable.

Most people thought that the worst thing that could happen to them was to become blind. Yet blind people were the most acceptable. Of the eight disabilities, the one thought to be the mildest was loss of hearing. Amputation was considered more normal and acceptable than any of the other disabilities. Artificial limbs seemed to the people questioned to replace the lost appearance and functioning power.

Physical deformations, hunchbacks and dwarves, evoked a feeling of evil and danger in the majority. Most in the survey said they would hide until they had some type of plastic surgery done on skin disorders.

But one of the strongest reactions of the survey was uncertainty. How does one behave toward the disabled? Should the disability be ignored? Would it be rude to ask how it happened, how the disabled person copes?

The sixties was a decade of questions from the able-bodied, of demands for rights by the disabled. The irony of the situation was that those who were able-bodied and asked the questions might in the very next moment by a stroke of fate become part of the disabled population. Thus there was an urgency for all citizens to understand the needs of the disabled.

The 1970s brought with it action by the disabled themselves. Activist organizations, such as Disabled in Action (DIA), National Association of Physically Handicapped (NAPH), Congress of Organizations of Physically Handicapped (COPH), became part of the political and social movement of the disabled that was sweeping the nation.

The disabled had survived the pioneering stage of the nineteen forties, the rehabilitation boom of the fifties, the frustration and self-exploration of the sixties. In the seventies, they decided it was time to do it themselves, time to become visual en masse, time to become vocal on issues that pertained to their survival, time to push for changes in legislation, time to show that a minority could affect the lives of the majority.

The disabled called for architects to take note of their needs in designing buildings that were to be accessible and in packaging their products. There was no practicality, for instance, in building a ramp to make a place accessible only to find out too late that the ramp was much too steep.

In the seventies, the Symbol of Access, designed to show which buildings have ramps or are accessible to wheelchairs, became a beacon of welcome to all who saw it. The symbol was seen in shopping centers, parking lots, state buildings, malls, courthouses; and behind each sign was the involvement of the disabled themselves.

The disabled supported civil rights legislation prohibiting discrimination against the handicapped. The legislation was slowly worked into the laws of individual states, but still had to be adopted by all states. The disabled urged that studies be made on transportation, education, housing, to show how inadequate these areas were when it came to the needs of those in wheelchairs.

THE NINETEEN SEVENTIES: MOMENTS TO REMEMBER

Colleges began to open up their campuses to disabled students. Airlines were challenged because of the unfair regulations that harassed the disabled traveler. Accessibility, legislation, and educating the able-bodied to a change of attitude became the quickened goals of the disabled. For the first time, they took their lives and their futures into their own hands.

But for many, no matter what other interests they involved themselves in, they would always return to wheelchair sports, to the rigid training schedules, to coaching, to keeping up with the changes in rules, in growth, and always the recruiting of new athletes.

In the early seventies, women began experimenting with wheelchair basketball. Wanting to do more than just compete in field and track events, they began to learn the

Ailene McCluney, a paraplegic, throwing the javelin at the Twentieth National Wheelchair Athletic Games, Farmingdale, New York, 1976.

complexities of the game. At first, the girls played against able-bodied players, as the men's teams had done at their beginning. Then, gradually, they sought out other women wheelchair teams that were beginning to organize. The Ms. Kids, one of the first teams, was started at the University of Illinois. The Detroit Ball Bearings hosted the first National Invitational Women's Wheelchair Basketball Tournament in Dearborn, Michigan. Women who did not belong to a team took advantage of the National Wheelchair Basketball Association's 1974 change in rules that permitted women to compete with men. The seventies would see women fighting for a division in the NWBA as they became a stronger force in all areas of wheelchair sports.

Sharon Myers, an exceptional woman athlete, was a familiar face at the Regionals in the seventies. The records she left behind would endure for many years.

Sharon became paralyzed at the age of three during a polio epidemic in 1950. She was cared for at home in Virginia, because the hospitals were filled at that time with hundreds of similar cases. Sharon's parents applied hot packs twice a day, and gradually, through exercises and constant attention, she regained movement in her arms.

Sharon's family encouraged her to try everything. During her childhood, she never remembers being told, "No, you aren't able to do that," even though she was in a wheelchair.

Her only slightly bitter memory that turns her blue eyes serious is that at first, because of her disability, she was not accepted in the public school system. Architectural barriers left another scar. And again . . . "I was told that the doors would be open for me to do whatever I wanted and was qualified to do after I finished school. After graduation, I found that the doors were open, but the steps leading to them were insurmountable."

At Woodrow Wilson Rehabilitation Center, for the first time, Sharon was able to play basketball, bowl, and learn to drive. (She had not been allowed to take gym in school; many schools prevent the disabled from taking gym classes because of their own misguided fears.)

The next move was wheelchair sports. After her first Nationals, Sharon came back eager to get others involved. A therapist at the center told her about a paraplegic who lifted weights. Sharon called him to share her excitement and to try to involve him in the wheelchair sports competition.

His name was Bill Myers, and they were married in December 1968. Bill designed and built their first home, and Sharon worked with the Easter Seal Society as director of Information and Referral.

Bill and Sharon, both blond-haired with sky-blue eyes, are young, enthusiastic, and totally involved in wheelchair sports. They have 1¼ acres of accessible ground on which they can practice field events—they even have an archery range. Before they bought the property, they purposely checked it out to make sure it was level and long enough for archery. In front of their house is a shot-put area. Sharon and Bill can train for sports events right in their own yard. The handsome couple encourage others just beginning wheelchair sports to come home with them, work out, share their land and their enthusiasm.

Bill, who was injured in a motorcycle accident several

years ago, has been captain of the United States Wheelchair Team and received the "Best Lifter Award." He has held the Pan American and National Lightweight Records.

There is a separate gym in back of the house where Bill does his weight lifting and where dozens of trophies are displayed.

Sharon works out at a nearby pool. There she also teaches children to swim. Sharon can do at least twenty-five lengths of the 25-yard pool without stopping. She finds it difficult to do the breaststroke, because she doesn't have normal muscle control in the back side of her arms. Yet she has won medals and broken records in breaststroke and backstroke. "In the water, I feel so independent," she says with her slow, southern way of speaking.

Sharon has seventy-eight first-place trophies, thirty-one second-place, and twenty-five third-place from regional, national, and international games. Most of these medals are for swimming, slalom, archery, pentathlon, 60-yard dash. Some also are for table tennis and basketball.

Bill and Sharon Myers work as a team, whether they are busy with Myers Equipment for the Handicapped (Bill installs all the equipment) or driving their tractor that has hand controls. Their home speaks out for the needs of the disabled, even to the accessible fireplace designed to bring a wheelchair close so that neither of them has a problem when putting on logs.

At one time Sharon and Bill Myers were the only competition from the state of Virginia. They would travel up to the Pennsylvania Regionals each year, making the eight-hour trip, just the two of them, representing Virginia. They were instrumental in forming the Virginia Wheelchair Athletic Association, which now has its own Regionals.

Sharon and Bill would arrive at the Regionals eager to share the growth and involvement of their particular state. The Regionals were catching on now. The successes of Stef Florescu and Charlie Ryder had encouraged others. Regional groups were popping up across the country. Through these new meets, wheelchair sports was reaching more athletes, more coaches, more officials, more audiences. In the late sixties and early seventies, regional meets were being held in California, Arizona, Maine, Pennsylvania, Michigan, Alabama, New Hampshire, and Massachusetts.

Now wheelchair athletes were beginning actively to recruit the disabled in their towns. They searched for men and women, perhaps young boys and girls at home, who had not heard about the Nationals or the Paralympics. It was the start of a journey to find the disabled and bring them out. The disabled were there waiting—in their homes, overprotected by parents who felt they were keeping their disabled loved ones safe from harm; in rehabilitation centers where coming back to life was the main goal; in institutions where doors had remained closed for too long.

The coaches and players talked to paraplegics and quadriplegics. They told their listeners of their travels, of the way the world of wheelchair sports had drawn them out to share experiences beyond their wildest hopes. They spoke at meetings and Y's and women's clubs and told of the free feeling of swimming, of the taunting teasing of the slalom, of the obstacles and ramps and platforms challenging the skill of the wheeler. They spoke to the parents of the disabled and tried to convince them that wheelchair sports was *not* the danger. The real danger was having the physically disabled sit at home inactive, not trying, unchallenged. The wheelchair sports advocates made appointments to talk to doctors, who were the first to see accident victims. It was urgent that doctors know the possibilities and benefits of sports participation.

A new magazine came out in the seventies. Its purpose— to speak for active wheelchair sports. *Sports 'n Spokes*, a magazine devoted exclusively to wheelchair sports and recreation, has as its publisher Cliff Crase, a star wheelchair athlete, and his wife, Nancy, a microbiologist. Cliff also is a constant contributor to *Paraplegia News*.

Cliff Crase has much firsthand experience to bring to his fledgling magazine. His exceptional record in wheelchair sports places him permanently in the pages of its history.

Clifford "Kip" Crase was in an automobile accident that left him paralyzed from the neck down. He came out of the accident with limited use of his right hand and full use of his left hand and arm. He had no movement in his legs.

Cliff had been an athlete before he became a quadriplegic. The most valuable player of his Rockland (Michigan) Prep basketball team, he had averaged 24 points a game. It was only natural that after his accident he return to sports. A coach Cliff knew suggested that he try swimming. The wheelchair, so new to him, made Cliff reluctant and a little fearful. The coach settled the matter by picking him up from the chair and throwing him into the pool. Cliff went under. When he came up, the handsome athlete was ready to rejoin the sports world.

Cliff swims the 25-meter backstroke in 38 seconds, the freestyle in 46, the breaststroke in 48, and he can "stride" his chair 40 yards in 12.5 seconds.

Honored as the first quadriplegic handicapped athlete of the year, Cliff has traveled extensively during his thirteen years in wheelchair sports. When he was captain of the United States team, he dined with the mayor of Vienna, Austria, met the president of Argentina, and was honored by accepting Her Majesty Queen Elizabeth of England's greeting to the United States team.

Cliff sports a golden-brown Arizona tan as he makes the rounds at the competitions, rounding up news for *Sports 'n Spokes,* which will in itself reach out and bring its readers deeper into the world where Cliff still competes. Cliff Crase believes not only in taking from wheelchair sports but in giving back, too.

The Wheelchair Sports Hall of Fame was formed in these early seventies, its purpose "to establish a permanent roster of those persons whose activities and conduct in wheelchair sports deserve the highest form of accolade." Those who were eligible were wheelchair athletes who had distinguished themselves in national and international competition through outstanding performance and superior sportsmanship. "Also, able-bodied or disabled individuals who had made significant contributions to wheelchair sports in administration, management, coaching, and/or promotion."

Wheelchair Sports Hall of Fame (National) Athletes

Alonzo Wilkins (deceased) 1970
Tim Harris, Helena, Mont. 1970

Ronald A. Stein, O'Fallon, Ill. 1970
Rosalie Hixson, Phoenixville, Pa. 1971
Jack Whitman, Champaign, Ill. 1971
Robert C. Hawkes, Bangor, Me. 1972
Denver Branum, Mt. Clemens, Mich. 1972
Clifford Crase, Phoenix, Ariz. 1973
Richard Maduro, Gainesville, Fla. 1973
Louis Rosini, Paoli, Pa. 1974
Stefan Florescu, Mich. 1975
Vincent Falardeau, Mass. 1976
Darlene Quinlan, Mich. 1977
William Fairbanks, Cal. 1977
Jim Mathis, Ohio 1977

Those who qualified as noncompetitors and who would be included in the National Wheelchair Sports Hall of Fame:

Benjamin H. Lipton, Malverne, N.Y. 1970
Timothy J. Nugent, Champaign, Ill. 1970
Seymour Bloom, Elmont, N.Y. 1971
Albert Youakim, Hillsdale, N.J. 1972
Ted McLean, Pearl River, N.Y. 1973
H. Charles Ryder, Mechanicsburg, Pa. 1974
Stan Labanowich, 1977

Denver Branum was elected to the Hall of Fame in 1972. It had been a long road for Denver from the Michigan YMCA where at the age of six he learned to swim and play basketball. It was there that he learned to compete and felt the pride of winning. It was also there that he learned of wheelchair sports.

Denver had been stricken with polio at the age of two. He had always competed with able-bodied players, determined to participate in sports despite his disability. Denver and his AB team had a dual meet with another YMCA whose athletic director knew Jack Leonard (then coach of the wheelchair basketball team, the Detroit Sparks). Jack asked Denver to join his team. The Detroit Sparks soon had a new player, and Denver Branum took his first step into wheelchair sports.

In track and field, his natural ability thrived after he returned from the National Wheelchair Games, setting new national records in swimming. In 1965, Denver won eight gold medals in the Stoke-Mandeville Games. Chosen 1974 Rookie of the Year, Denver also captured the title of most valuable player in the National Wheelchair Basketball Tournament.

Superathletes like Denver were igniting the response of audiences. Their success encouraged others to form new teams and to leave their marks.

In the early seventies, there were eleven state and invitational regionals to choose from. One thousand competitors had become active.

Crowds of disabled were showing up at the New York Nationals wherever they were held. Those who had been among the original sixty-five competitors at the first Adelphi Nationals couldn't believe the swarm of wheelchairs that were in the hotel lobby the weekend of competition. The names on the jackets of the players whizzed by—the Silver Streaks, the Rochester Rebels, the Central Penn Wheelers, the Gizz Kids, the Delaware Valley Spokesmen, Penn Chariot Racers ... some with their big sombreros, others with Indian headbands, long hair, and beads . . . each team in its own way breaking out of the stereotype that all disabled are alike.

Because of the great influx of competitors at the Nationals, there was a change of rules in 1972. It became impossible to accommodate the hundreds that flocked to New York City. Now it was necessary to limit the Nationals by having the athletes qualify at the Regionals in order to attend the Nationals as competitors.

With the new qualifying Regionals, fewer would make it to New York, but with more Regionals still forming around the country, there was more chance for competition on a state level. The focus was no longer on one trip a year, though it still remained an incentive. The qualifying process spurred on the formation of smaller teams within cities and states, and gave wheelchair sports an internal strength it never had before.

During the weekends of regional and national competition, while javelin and discus and arrow flew through the air, all else was forgotten—the unemployment, the unacceptance, the discrimination, the loneliness. Skill, determination, challenge, and the rewards of persistent training were all that remained.

Young people were drawn to the athletes whether on the basketball courts or in the field. Children would run up playfully and jump into a player's lap. A waiting athlete, lying on a field ground, catching a fleeting rest, would see his wheelchair being driven by a walking six-year-old, trying it out. Teen-agers, followers of the teams, would find their lifelong ambition taking hold out there, somewhere between the watching and the waiting. Many would come away knowing someday they would become physical therapists, recreational therapists, gym instructors. There was no self-consciousness felt by the young toward the wheelchair athlete—just respect and wonder.

Wrapped in blankets, while the chill of early spring nipped at the athletes, the competitors sipped hot coffee as markers were checked and coaches and athletes huddled together in kinship. A circle of closeness, of family, spread its touch from wheelchair to wheelchair, no matter what city or state, no matter what color, no matter what type of disability. It was a circle of sharing, one that few outside it would understand.

Regional competitors and Regional hoppers (those who traveled from Regional to Regional) were eager to share the growth and involvement of their particular state. Much information was exchanged at the meets. At the Regionals, athletes found out how things were going in Florida; what Arizona was doing about transportation for the disabled; if Nassau was getting more competitors than last year. And all about Iowa, Michigan, California, Pennsylvania, Washington, Ohio, Illinois, Virginia, Oregon, Colorado, Minnesota, and New England—where Regionals were being held.

The weight lifters, with their muscles bulging, shared their training schedules, told of their special diets and countless hours lifting weights.

One of the greatest weight lifters of all times is Lou Rosini. Lou began lifting weights seriously at a VA hospital as a result of his rehabilitation program. He was one of the earlier basketball players in the VA Hospital in 1950.

Lou's parents came from Italy. His dad brought with him the skill of carpentry. Lou watched him and learned, and he continues the craft today.

In high school, Lou became involved in football and weight lifting. After he graduated, he took a job as a track man on the railroad.

During the Korean War, Lou served forty months in the infantry. As a platoon sergeant, he was caught in an enemy ambush and joined the ranks of the physically disabled.

Lou has beautiful memories of wheelchair sports which he holds closely to him. A quiet man, he speaks easily of the wheelchair sports exhibition he was part of for President Kennedy's Employment of the Handicapped Committee in Hershey, Pennsylvania. The VA administration of the Pennsylvania area asked Lou to get together a basketball demonstration game to be played at the conference. Lou gathered a few players he knew and some who were sent to him.

The wheelchair basketball demonstration was to be the birth of wheelchair sports in Pennsylvania. The team was called the Paranauts. Lou became their coach and player.

Lou began weight lifting seriously at the first Nationals. He won in the heavyweight division, lifting three hundred pounds. In 1970, he raised four hundred pounds to win the national heavyweight title. In the Paralympics, he would hold the title of second in the world and would return with three Pan American records. Lou held an undefeated record of eight consecutive years in the Nationals from 1963 to 1971.

Hailing from West Philadelphia, Lou is six feet tall; he

is married and has one daughter. His wife and daughter know the dedication Lou has given weight lifting, and they share in his training efforts.

Before a meet, no one is able to talk to him. For about a week, the strong handsome face closes itself off. Inside is turmoil, outside is calm, as Lou prepares for contest. During that time, he feels the self-determination to win— nothing more, nothing less. He goes over the proper position of his hands, the breathing, the timing. All his thoughts are focused on the meet ahead.

Lou, who also held a national shot-put record, trains eleven months a year. During a single training session, he lifts thousands of pounds or he does fifty repetition lifts, lifting different weights. He trains two hours a day, and tries to hit his limit only once a month. One day a month, he reenacts a total meet situation which is the warm-up, then three of his best lifts.

Lou's eyes grow hard and the strong lines of his face tighten when he speaks of the people he has little time for, such as those "do-for-me" disabled who sit back, "waiting for recovery."

He warms to people who are independent, who after a traumatic accident make something of their lives. The big man with the soft-spoken voice admires Swimmer Al Alcocer who has set swimming records in individual medley, breaststroke, backstroke. But it's not just the record-breaking ability of Al "Cochise" Alcocer that Lou admires. It's that Al trains by swimming ten miles a day. Cochise, a double-amputee Vietnam vet, reaches home from the Nationals and immediately starts training for the next year.

Dedication and performance are the qualities that win Lou's admiration. Lou Rosini is far more comfortable talking about someone else than about himself.

Part of the excitement at the Nationals is in learning, in appreciating the dedication of the other athletes. The swimmers tell of their constant training in pools all winter, practicing the backstroke, the breaststroke, the front free-stroke, bobbing, learning breathing exercises.

Judy Benoit is one of those swimmers. A Class II paraplegic, Judy's life has been a sequence of changes that took her from the state of Maryland to Hawaii.

Judy discovered wheelchair sports at the University of Illinois. She participated in swimming, field events, and table tennis. But it was in swimming and table tennis that she captured her silver and gold medals.

A competitor since 1964, Judy brought back from the Paralympics the following year three silver medals in swimming: front freestyle, back freestyle, and breaststroke. In 1966, she traveled to Jamaica with a demonstration team and later won two gold medals in front freestyle and breaststroke. Her proudest moments came in 1974 and 1975 when she held the national record in breaststroke and individual medley.

With sharp, piercing blue eyes and long blond hair, Judy is five feet tall, petite, and fiercely independent. Sports is only a part of her life. Though she has traveled around a lot, the "me" in Judy, her inner being, finds affirmation in her creative outlets—antiquing, refinishing furniture, putting an apartment together. The "me" in

Judy is what she leaves in everything she touches and what she refuses to give up.

Hawaii didn't have a wheelchair sports team until Judy Benoit journeyed there to live. She helped organize its first team in 1974, when Hawaii held its first "Aloha Games" regional qualifying meet. The meets raised enough money to take thirteen qualifying athletes to the eighteenth National Wheelchair Games in Cheney, Washington.

Honored as Sportswoman of the Day and of the Week by a Hawaii local radio station, Judy Benoit became the first president of the Hawaii Wheelchair Athletic Association. The association encourages sporting activities throughout the year. It hopes to develop sports skills and encourages neighboring island residents to participate.

Holder of five Hawaii state records, Judy at one time wrote a column about wheelchair sports from the woman's angle for the sports page of *Paraplegia News*.

Some athletes traveled alone to the competitions. Others brought their coaches. The role of the coach to the wheelchair athlete was one of teacher, brother, father, and friend. The coach was often the link between the able-bodied and the disabled, and the relationship was the finest example of the combined efforts of the two, the working together of legs and minds, of skill and knowledge, of faith and persistence. The coach often got it together and kept it together. His bond with his team was tight—with equal parts of authority and love.

The coach was the one who rounded up the athletes the night before competition, so that they would be rested and at their best the next day. He was also the one on the field who sweated out the decisions, who fretted over each performance thinking maybe he had done too little or too much. The coach came with his athletes, supporting them, guiding them, sometimes pushing them during the long grueling hours of training and competition past his own physical powers of endurance.

Coach Kenneth C. Clarke (Casey), who was the director of recreation and athletics at the University of Illinois Rehabilitation Center, had this to say to his wheelchair athletes: "Take care of your wheelchairs. They are as sacred to paraplegic athletes as racing cars are to racing drivers."

Many will recall Casey's first trip to the Nationals in 1960. He was coach with the Gizz Kids, the exciting wheelchair sports team from the University of Illinois. The university had sent Casey and his Gizz Kids east, seeking victory.

It had taken twenty-four hours on the bus to reach New York, and all had spent a sleepless night. Yet Casey and the Kids rushed eagerly out to see the city they had only heard of or read about before.

The 240-yard shuttle-relay with Class I and Class II competing was the last event of the weekend. Paul Sones, the anchorman on the relay team for the Gizz Kids, was destined to start out behind in the race.

The audience suddenly scattered, running for shelter to the adjacent Bulova Building, as a summer shower drenched the track and the three wheelchair relay teams in the finals. Casey Clarke was drenched as well as he watched Paul Sones pressing forward with the water driving against his face, pushing and pushing, his thumbs pressed on both his tires as well as the hard rim of his wheels for a better grip. Paul Sones pushed on past the leading team's anchorman, a gold medalist in the earlier dashes, to a joyous victory.

It was a victory for the Illinois Gizz Kids, a team that had won as a team. It was a victory for an athlete named Paul Sones, a private triumph over pressure in competition that not even the rain could drive away. And it was a victory for a coach named Kenneth C. Clarke who was taking home a national championship.

Casey did more than bring the Gizz Kids to the Nationals those many years ago. He brought news to New York of a new program he and others were forming out in Illinois. Casey's program took a nonathlete, and in three to four weeks trained him or her to match the performance of an achieving athlete. Until the success of this program, it was thought that only former athletes could achieve in wheelchair sports. But through diligent training, through sophisticated coaching programs, men such as Clarke opened up competition in wheelchair sports to all disabled who were willing to put in the time to train and who would take their competitions seriously.

Another Casey victory was the 1963 Stoke-Mandeville Games in England. He, as coach, and Tim Harris, a wheelchair athlete, led the Gizz Kids to victory, scoring 172 points of the United States team's winning total of 331. Scoring over half of the total United States team's points, the Gizz Kids numbered but seven of the thirty-six men and women squad. Tim Harris, new to wheelchair sports, proved an inspiration to the Gizz Kids as he captured one

Top: *Olaf Hurd, a paraplegic, table-tennis gold medalist at the 1975 Virginia Regionals, 1976 silver medalist. (Photo 1976, Woodrow Wilson Rehabilitation Center, Fisherville, Virginia.)*

Right: *Mike Dempsey, paraplegic, United States Table Tennis Champion. (Photo 1976, National Wheelchair Athletic Games.)*

Coach Lou Neishloss and his wife Genie Neishloss, who had polio. (Photo 1976)

Quadriplegic Skip Wilkins, using the special "quad" bowling stick and ball with retractable handle. (Photo 1976 at Woodrow Wilson Rehabilitation Center.)

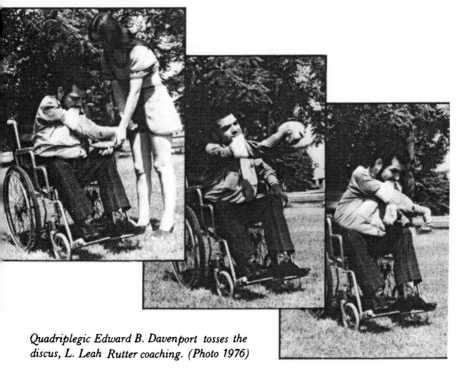

Quadriplegic Edward B. Davenport tosses the discus, L. Leah Rutter coaching. (Photo 1976)

medal after another in swimming, field events, basketball, and weight lifting. The Kids brought home the pentathlon trophy that year, which is equal in prestige and importance to the decathlon in the regular Olympics.

K. C. Clarke believes that if a disabled athlete keeps his shoulders and wrists in good shape, he can play wheelchair sports indefinitely throughout his life. He seeks always to keep competition a joy and excelling a moment of personal triumph.

Many families of the physically disabled were concerned about their young people being introduced to the speed of the races, the daredevil maneuvering of wheelchairs, the rubbing and tipping, leaving blistering hands, the thundering across the basketball courts. Casey talked to parents whenever he could. He explained to them that serious injury in wheelchair sports is virtually nonexistent. Even in wheelchair football, where offensive halfback and defensive safety collide at speeds of ten miles an hour, the athlete is protected from body contact by the frame of the wheelchair. Wheelchair athletes are taught how to fall out of a wheelchair safely and how to get back in. This knowledge is carried over to dating and daily living. Wheelchair Libbers, as Casey fondly calls them, gain better balance and find a new independence from the training and challenges that competition presents.

The year that the Illinois Gizz Kids and Casey Clarke came home with a championship they brought with them 40 percent of the medals. They left behind them the knowledge and experience that they had collected. They left it for others to build on. That is what wheelchair sports is all about.

Young faces joined the Regionals, and among them a fresh, bright energetic new team called the Central Penn Wheelers. Its coach was Lou Neishloss, an AB, the man who taught Rosie Hixson to swim.

Lou, a native of Norristown, Pennsylvania, first became interested in the disabled while working at a summer job and going to college. One of the guests asked Lou to teach their daughter how to swim. He said yes, before knowing that the girl was in a wheelchair. For a moment, when he realized that the girl was disabled, he grew apprehensive, uncertain. It was these emotions that later stayed with him and led him to wonder just how many disabled were out there, able and yearning to swim. The girl, a nine-year-old high-level paraplegic, learned to swim that summer because of Lou. He supported her in the water by her chin, at first showing her the proper arm movements. He let her swim a couple of feet, then a couple of yards.

Later, Lou became a physical-education instructor at the Pennsylvania Rehabilitation Center in Johnstown. There he developed a sports program that in 1964 took many of his team to Japan. Lou went as coach of the United States girls' team that competed in the Paralympics.

Coach Neishloss experimented with isotonic and isometric studies. If a discus thrower could throw six inches farther with a stronger supporting muscle, Lou had the athlete develop that particular muscle.

Lou's BVR Wheelers of Johnstown won a national championship. During his stay at Johnstown, Lou felt the only way to find out how someone felt in a wheelchair was to experience it himself. He spent an hour a day in a wheelchair almost every day for a couple of years.

Lou returned to Norristown, Pennsylvania, and formed the Central Penn Wheelers. From 1968 through 1972 his girls' team won the state championship four times in a row.

Neishloss made it a practice never to ask an athlete to do anything that he didn't do himself. If he asked someone to push a mile in a wheelchair, he'd push a mile, too. Central Penn Wheelers went on to win two Nationals and to compete regularly in the Paralympics. And Lou, who went into wheelchair sports because he saw people reaching out for life, continues to develop superior athletes wherever he goes.

The seventies would see a very quiet coach enter almost on tiptoe, so quietly he came, yet this gentle man would have an impact on wheelchair sports that would be felt around the world. Jim Messer's involvement came from his own personal experience as a youth.

At the age of thirteen, Jim contracted typhoid fever. Two months in a hospital left him weakened and unable to attend school for three additional months. There were many hours to take walks, to think, and to read. Time grew heavy for the once active body. To pass the hours, Jim got a book on physical training. Through exercise and running, he was able to regain his health, but he still remained underweight.

And then he discovered weights. He was eighteen when he started weight-lifting and though still thin, he began to set records. Jim competed and sometimes acted as an official until 1933 when he traveled to Chicago for the National Weight Lifting Championships, where he acted for the first time as an official for a national contest. Jim then took his talents to the Holy Saviour Club, in Norristown, Pennsylvania, where he coached weight-lifters.

Jim met Lou Neishloss, then coach of the Central Penn Wheelers. The two men developed exercise programs for the Wheelers, exercises that would develop their muscle strength, improve their health, and give them better endurance for national competition. The training program helped bring Central Penn its victory for the women's team in the Nationals.

During this time, Jim designed and developed a weight-training bench and telescopic stand, which are now being used in the weight-lifting part of the wheelchair games, both in national and international competition. Before Jim's invention, paraplegics used to lift from a mat on the floor. This could prove dangerous if the weights were dropped. Jim's weight-training bench has two telescopic stands, one on each side, which can be raised or lowered. Should the lifter fail to lift the weight, it will fall back on the stand, not the lifter.

Paraplegics can't walk. Their arms are their legs for the rest of their lives. Through barbell and dumbbell exercises, Jim guided hundreds of physically disabled to strengthening their upper bodies to better performance. He also corresponded with paraplegics and assisted them in their training by getting equipment for them.

He and Lou Rosini, retired heavyweight champion, developed a program to train officials for the weight-lifting competition in the National Wheelchair Games. Because of these two men, officials would have to take a test and officiate at several contests before they are qualified officials.

Jim knows that everyone can't be a lifter because one's

body structure might not be suitable, but he believes that anybody can keep fit by some weight training. He'd like to see more girls, especially those with physical disabilities, lift weights. He has encouraged girls to use the barbells and dumbbells for upper body exercises and to work out in the many weight-lifting clubs that are unused several evenings a week, across the country.

Wheelchair athletes display the most spectacular upper-body builds ever seen. The men, with muscles rippling, are products of training programs such as Jim's. The girls, full-bosomed and graceful, have had the benefit of fine coaches, coaches who searched and are still searching for new techniques, coaches like Jim Messer.

Another record-breaking athlete, Julius Duval, travels to hospitals to seek out the newly disabled, introducing them to wheelchair sports and gradually bringing them back to the outside world.

He likes to tell interested friends and fans how he trained a guy in shot put to beat him, and he did. It was the best loss that Julius ever had. One of nine sisters and three brothers, Julius comes from a proud, strong-minded family, and perhaps because of that strength, he prides himself in being independent and quite stubborn. Julius is a quadriplegic. His dark brooding eyes will sweep you in if you allow them. He talks easily of his desire to be loved by his competitors and fans. "We, the disabled, must believe the world is still ours," he says.

A high school dropout, Julius will at the age of twenty-eight be graduating from high school and going on to college, so that some day he can teach those with disabilities. "Everyone," he says, "eventually has to get his act together."

Julius Duval cares about wheelchair sports; he cares about others; he cares about caring.

Robert Hawkes cares about eagles—bald eagles—becoming extinct, because pollution and man are destroying this great symbol of our country. He watches them from his window in Bangor, Maine—and then in the mornings he feeds the wild life: birds, chipmunks, red squirrels. Sometimes deer walk by. This champion athlete used to be a hunter. "It's much more pleasant to watch live animals in their play and courtship, than lifeless, with all their beauty and grace removed." And so he hunts no more.

Robert Hawkes was injured while attempting to reduce the falling velocity of a collapsing hay conveyor because of children in the area nearby. He is a paraplegic.

Robert is president of the Independent Living Center for "quads." The Independent Living Center provides attendants and aids for quadriplegics so that they can attend school or have on-the-job training. One "quad" now living at the center had been living in a nursing home with senile and terminal patients, yet the boy's age was only nineteen. Now he is able to explore sports, recreation, vocational possibility, college courses, and perhaps one day, wheelchair sports.

Whether it be feeding bald eagles because he believes in bald eagles, or helping people because he believes in people, Robert Hawkes does not stand aside and talk about what should be done. He just does it. As a member of ten

Paralympic team competitions, his record in wheelchair sports stands with the great ones.

Always, each year, at the Nationals along with the familiar faces come the new ones, staking out their own territory, finding their own path.

Bonita Reed, a paraplegic, came to her first Nationals recently at nineteen. She broke a national discus record, leaving her mark, 43 feet 3⅝ inches. Bonita can be found at Woodrow Wilson Rehabilitation Center taking courses as a clerk-typist keypunch trainee.

Alfred T. Wilkins, Jr., known to friends as Skip, fills his hours as director of a crisis intervention center. Competing just three years in Class IA, Skip holds a national record in 1976 shot put with 14 feet 5¾ inches.

Skip, who is twenty-six-years-old, had numerous football scholarships offered him when he was seventeen. Hurt in water skiing, he believes the Lord prepared him to use his competitive skills directly and persistently in wheelchair sports.

Wilma Walker, sixteen, in her second year at the Nationals, won first place in discus, setting a new 1976 national record, 53 feet 5¼ inches. She won first place in javelin with 41 feet 3¼ inches, and second place in shot. Wilma became disabled in a bicycle accident. Traveling from Lawrence, Kansas, she, her father, and brother gathered in victory on the fields of the Nationals. Her practice area at home is the park across the street from where she lives.

One day Ronda July could walk and then the next day she couldn't. "But it was still me," she says emphatically. A beautiful, restless, active girl, Ronda took a tumble from a horse and became a paraplegic. A student at the University of Illinois, Ronda captured the attention of those at the Nationals with her splendid shooting ability in archery. With the philosophy that "it's the now in life that counts," she can be counted among the exciting new faces.

Derry Dale Sadler of Denver, Colorado, flew in from Colorado, on his first trip, left his mark in discus, 123 feet, 7 inches, and javelin, 93 feet. A deputy district attorney, Sadler becomes a different person when in the pit throwing. A fierceness, a thrust of energy, a rush seems to flow through his body as the concentration, the hours of training are clearly marked in every straining line of his face. Just like a volcano erupting on the field, Dale lets go with his throw, and the sports enthusiasts applaud his skill.

"I knew that I was paralyzed. It just felt as if my body was floating." Chris Lambruscati fell from a practice tower while watching her brother sky-dive. A sky-dive enthusiast herself, she came away from the accident a quadriplegic. A picture to watch in competition, auburn hair picking up tinges of the sun, a strikingly lovely face concentrating, Chris soon picked up her own crew of fans. Medal winner in discus, javelin, 40-yard dash, wheelchair slalom, backstroke, club throwing, and shot put, Chris continues her daredevil drive to win. Tomorrow . . . maybe the Paralympics . . . maybe even sky-diving again.

New styles come along with the new faces—different ways of swimming, of throwing, of shooting archery.

Katie Adams thrilled the audiences at the 1976 Nationals with her archery technique. Katie came to the competitions from Connecticut with her instructor Craig Huber. Craig started training Katie two years before. Katie suffers from arthrogryposis, a form of arthritis, which has affected her hands and legs. But still she chose to compete in archery—and compete and hit the gold bull's-eye she did. The bow is held by Katie's feet. She uses her right foot for lateral aim. She tells Craig how to position the bow, up or down. Katie pulls back with two fingers on her right hand and then lets go. Judgment is from eyes to foot to target. There must be a kinesthetic awareness for this to succeed. Katie moves her right leg to adjust the bow from side to side. She moves her leg up and down for height. Katie stunned the audiences with her archery and brought a new and exciting technique to the Nationals.

Throughout the competitions, mingling with the new faces, new styles, old champions and new ones, are the helpers, the young people from colleges, young therapists, friends, family who come to watch, to retrieve javelins, to carry equipment.

Daniel Barth, red-faced, sunburned, sweating, blond hair wet and hitting his forehead, tired but content from lugging, was in constant motion the entire weekend of the 1976 Nationals. Nineteen-year-old Barth came to aid his friend, athlete Ken Cunningham. Barth carried the equipment. Ken Cunningham, who has muscular dystrophy, didn't win, but he learned and will be back. Both of them will probably be back. Daniel Barth is getting something out of the competitions, too. He can't quite put it into words, but he feels it inside. It has something to do with being Ken's right-hand man, about being needed; it's tied in with a good feeling that comes from a lot of hard work and a feeling of comradeship.

L. Leah Rutter has long dark hair folding over her shoulders. A graduate in specialized education, she takes notes, assists quadriplegic Edward B. Davenport, organizes Quad Squad (a wheelchair sports team for quadriplegics), gets drinks, packs suitcases, loads and unloads cars, her legs making up for dozens that can't walk. Quiet, gentle Leah, as constant as the next summer, is a helper, without whom many could not even reach the games.

Though many of the athletes have traveled to the Nationals for over fifteen years, it is different every time, and it is that constant change that brings them back time and time again. Each year something is added, or something happens, something different or unexpected that awes the crowds and even surprises the competitors themselves.

Who could forget the night that the dance was held, the dance for the wheelchair athletes? Rock music bounced off the walls. The room shook with rhythm, wheelchair clicking, silhouettes against the shadows, crutches, braces, wheels becoming invisible as only the music mattered. Six girls in wheelchairs with bows in their hair, forming a chorus line, their puffed short-bloused sleeves moving with their bodies, gracefully dancing in their wheelchairs. Amputees did wheelies, while pretty girls sat in their laps holding on for dear life. It was just a dance for young people. And young people danced. To the disabled, that's all it was.

Not too long ago, at the Pennsylvania Regionals, Edward B. Davenport, a quadriplegic, felt that quadriplegics had a potential that hadn't been recognized at the games. So he set out to prove what he could do. He had fought for several years to put the 220-yard dash in the Regionals. The competition for quadriplegics thus far had been the 40- and 60-yard dash.

Quadriplegics are not in the same class as paraplegics when it comes to speed. Quads have physical limitations in their arms and hands. It had been felt that because of this limited power, the longer distance races would exhaust the quadriplegic athlete. Ed had argued that quads had endurance and could take longer runs. The year the Regionals said yes, Ed entered the competition. He analyzed the track before the race and decided what pace he would set for himself. Only five quads were involved and the big question in everyone's mind was, Could they finish?

Ed lagged behind in third place. And then something happened. It was as though a small clock started to tick inside him. With only limited power in his hands and arms, he began to spin the wheels faster and faster. With 60 yards to go until the finish line, Ed passed the second man, and then with the crowd now caught up in the desperate push he was making, he passed the leader. The officials broke out in a roar as the crowd exploded. The air was filled with shouting, and caps were tossed high as Ed Davenport opened up a new area of competition for quads in this country.

And then there was the time at the Nationals when a guy named Tom McLaughlin, a quad with one arm missing, decided to swim the pool. Tom had already become famous at the Nationals for his unique way of throwing the javelin. He didn't have triceps to depend on, and the muscles in the back of the arm that are ordinarily used for straightening were useless to him. But he did have the power of biceps. Using that power, he developed his own method of throwing the javelin with his back to the field, throwing it over his shoulder.

The shouts would become contagious, "Tommy's ready to throw," and everyone at the games would rush hurriedly to the spot. Sometimes when the rain and wind blew against his face, dozens would brave the weather just to see him do it one more time.

But it was the night that Tommy swam the length of the pool that everyone would remember. It was in 1971. Most swimmers would clear the pool in fifty seconds or less. But Tommy, using his one arm, took over two minutes to swim the length of the pool. Toward the end, he grew tired, and the crowd sensed his fatigue, his struggle. They all stood and clapped and called his name, shouting, "You can do it Tommy. You can make it," applauding his courage, letting him know that it mattered that he finish. It mattered to everyone present.

And when he did finish, when he reached the other end of the pool, the audience stood for five minutes, applauding him in an ovation that wheelchair sports would long remember.

The moments to remember are always there . . . like the time John Panatieri tossed the discus into the air and established a record of 126 feet that would remain unbroken for years to come . . . and the time John Martin, only 98 pounds himself, lifted 275 pounds in weight lifting. The heartache memories would be there, too. The weekend that the Central Penn Girls' team had won the trophy for two years (three years and it would be theirs to keep) and that third year, that heartbreaking weekend, they lost it by a quarter of a point to the University of Illinois. There would be moments of frustration, like the time the teams were booked into a motel and none of the wheelchairs could fit into the bathrooms, or the time they found steps leading up to the main restaurant.

And there would be the new moments, every day, every week, every month, when an athlete would emerge, opening up a new area of sports to the disabled. Jack Robertson, a paraplegic from Elyria, Ohio, challenged the churning waters of the English Channel, swimming all but 500 yards of it. Bruce Jennings, an amputee with one leg, took a 3,000-mile coast-to-coast bicycle ride across the United States. And in 1977, Bobby Hall, David Williamson, and Curt Brinkman entered the National Wheelchair Marathon, held in conjunction with the Boston Marathon, three out of the seven wheelchair athletes (one of whom, Sharon Rahn, was a woman) who participated. Bobby Hall, polio in one leg, finished the race, 26 miles—385 yards—in 2 hours and 40 minutes. David Williamson, polio-paraplegic, finished in 3 hours and 20 minutes. Both finished in the top third of all the entries in the Boston Marathon. All wheelchair entries finished the race.

But more important than memories is the talk of the future, the charting of hopes and plans for the disabled and for wheelchair sports. Some of the hopes are important and specific:

That surveys will be taken in townships, counties, cities, and states so that the physically disabled can be counted and brought into the world and into wheelchair sports.

That voting booths will have voting levers lowered or fitted with adaptable devices so that a wheelchair citizen can vote in private.

That halfway houses or transition centers will be built, acting as partners to rehabilitation centers.

That there will be better medical and dental care.

That there will be adequate transportation, suitable housing, and designers, engineers, and architects who will meet the challenge of creating a building that all people can enter.

That there will be more curb cuts, more ramps, and less ignorance.

That wheelchair sports will expand, taking in more competitors, more competitions, more countries, and gaining the interest and support of more able-bodied citizens in this country.

Meanwhile, there is no time to lose. New athletes are opening up new areas of wheelchair sports, new areas of thought, daring to push away stereotypes, taking trains and cars and planes to compete, pushing their bodies past fatigue, past disability, sometimes past disease, to achieve.

Our country has always had its ambassadors. But a new sort of ambassador has been emerging over the years, one who travels throughout the world representing this country's outlook toward the physically disabled—our vital, skillful, pioneering ambassadors of wheelchair sports.

The pencil-thin outline of a figure resting on a wheel is officially recognized as the international Symbol of Access. Wherever it is shown, from whatever window it appears, in department stores, restrooms, or parking lots, the disabled know that they may enter without the complications of architectural barriers. The Symbol of Access is an invitation to the physically disabled to enter.

In 1968, Rehabilitation International, an international society for rehabilitation of the disabled, appointed a panel composed of representatives of international architectural-design and graphic organizations. Members of the panel, those involved and concerned with the disabled, were to select a design both simple and aesthetic that would clearly identify barrier-free areas.

The Scandinavian Design Students Organization came up with a contribution, and the International Symbol of Access is a modification of their design. The symbol was adopted in 1969 by the Assembly of Rehabilitation International.

The Symbol of Access is a reminder that too many buildings and much of life has been closed to the disabled for too long. Those who display the symbol are those who are looking toward the future, for the symbol is a sign of a changing society and a move toward enlightenment. Those who display it will be the pioneers in a new move sweeping the country and touching all parts of the world.

Friends and teammates of quadriplegic Debbie Russell congratulate her after her record-breaking shot-put toss at the National Wheelchair Athletic Games, 1976.

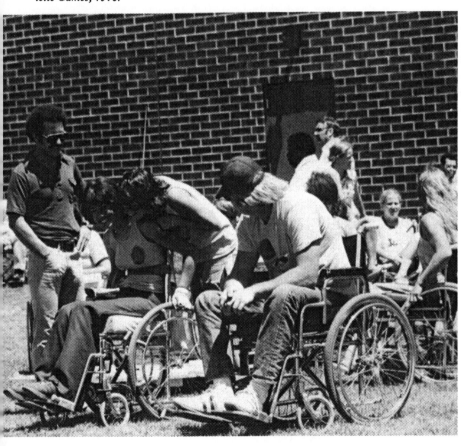

If You Were Suddenly Disabled . . .

Could you get into your school?
Could you get into your own home?
Could you, in the wheelchair, use the restroom at your place of
  business?
Could you go to your local movie house?
Could you get through the doorway of your best friend's house?
Could you get into your favorite restaurant?
Which sports would you have to give up?
Could you get on a bus in your community?
Could you get into a voting booth?
Could you join a wheelchair team in your community?
Could you join a disabled activist organization in your
  community?

Look at your home, at your school, at your community and
ask yourself what you could do to make it accessible. What areas
could be equipped with ramps? What doorways could be wid-
ened? How could your local supermarkets be made accessible?

Get in a wheelchair for a day. You will quickly learn that you
have to think ahead. Is that a left turn or a right? Does the door
in front push in or pull out? Can the wheelchair cross that curb?

If you were suddenly disabled, you might find that the world
you knew was just inches away—but out of your reach.

For Further Information on Wheelchair Sports—Records, History, Standings, and Rules—Write to the Following Organizations:

National Wheelchair Athletic Association
40-24 62nd Street
Woodside, New York 11377

National Wheelchair Basketball Association
110 Seaton Bldg., University of Kentucky
Lexington, Kentucky 40506

American Wheelchair Bowling Association
2635 Northeast 19th Street
Pompano Beach, Florida 33062

Paralyzed Veterans of America
7315 Wisconsin Avenue, Suite 301-W
Washington, D.C. 20014

Publications

Directory of Organizations Interested in the Handicapped
Committee for the Handicapped
People to People Program
Suite 610, LaSalle Building
Connecticut Ave. and L. St.
Washington, D.C. 20036

Rights of the Physically Handicapped:
A Layman's Guide to the Law
Edited by Mick Joyce
Rehabilitation Service Dept.
Southwest State University, Marshall, Minnesota

INDEX

(Page numbers in italic indicate photographs.)

ABOUT THE AUTHOR

Harriet May Savitz is a woman who cares about many things, and her writing is a direct result of her interests. In addition to WHEELCHAIR CHAMPIONS, she has written several novels, including *Fly, Wheels, Fly!, The Lionhearted,* and *On the Move,* which reflect her most important concerns—those of the physically disabled. Her books are, in her own words, "about the change in attitude amongst the disabled population. They're about people of courage who want the rights long kept out of their reach ... the rights of transportation, accessibility, education, social acceptance, and understanding."

Harriet Savitz travels with wheelchair sports teams to all national competitions, is a member of the National Wheelchair Athletic Association, and cofounder of Veep, an organization to help and inform the disabled. She lives with her husband and two children in Plymouth Meeting, Pennsylvania.

Harriet May Savitz received the Outstanding Author Award, Pennsylvania School Library Association 1981.

www.harrietmaysavitz.com   hmaysavitz@aol.com

Whenever it is spring, I think of the Wheelchair Games and those who competed in them. For years I traveled with many of the teams, writing in books what I experienced in wheelchair sports. Wherever we visited, in whatever motel or hotel, or restaurant, we had to deal with steps, narrow doorways and uncomfortable expressions of other people. Wherever we traveled, we reminded others that accessibility and attitudes were the problems, not the disabled.

Wheelchair sports brought the disabled out into the community in masses. In the years since the publication of this first history of the athletes and trainers, the coaches and therapists, of all the pioneers in this disabled movement, there has been a steady development of sports involving the disabled and an expansion of the competitions. Throughout these past years, I have received numerous requests for this book by trainers, therapists, teachers, librarians, and the disabled themselves. I feel now as I felt then when I wrote the book, that each generation should know the struggles and accomplishments of the pioneers who determined that the disabled could establish themselves as self-fulfilled active citizens.

Nothing has been changed in the text. Jim McGowan, the photographer for the first printing, himself a quadriplegic-amputee, offered the original cover for the book. Wheelchair Champions is a history of the courageous and determined disabled and able-bodied who dared to believe that those in wheelchairs could be competitive in sports as well as in all areas of life.

Harriet May Savitz—2006

Please note the references to organizations and suggested reading material in the back of this book are outdated. Now new sources can be found in the wonderful world of the Internet.

978-0-595-38522-5
0-595-38522-2

Lightning Source UK Ltd.
Milton Keynes UK
UKOW04f1702310114

225660UK00001B/34/A